THE SCHOOL FOR
WICKED
WITCHES
WICKED ON THE WIND
WILL TAYLOR
SCHOLASTIC

ISBN 978-93-5954-432-8

Printed in India at Acme Print O Pac. Pvt. Ltd. Noida

This reprint editon: September 2025
Book design by Meve Norton

FOR THE KIDS STILL LOOKING.

YOUR MAGIC WILL FIND ITS HOME.

1

VIVIENNE

Vivienne Morderay turned the final page of the book resting on her marble table, closed it, and leaned back in her chair, her mouth curling into a smile so wicked it would rot soap.

She reached out a pale lilac hand and patted the little green cover. The book—a user manual for the Lost Collar of Arboc—had exceeded her wildest expectations, and she finally had it memorized.

Vivienne did not know who Arboc was, or if they had been the one to make the collar or write the book. Frankly, she didn't care. The completed collar was hers now after a lifetime of searching. With the secrets contained in this precious tome, she had just become unstoppable.

Even the title, *Volatilium Gemmis,* made her smile. According to another of her books, that translated to both *flying jewels* and *birds of prey*. It was all so deliciously perfect.

Vivienne exhaled through her diamond-crusted lips, surprised to feel a tremendous calm rising inside her. She had yearned for this moment since the cold, rainy morning she'd been sent away to school as a child. Back then she'd been just one more North Oz girl bundled into the Wicked Wagon as she and her unwanted magic were sent out of sight and out of mind. Now she had everything she'd ever wanted: beauty, fame, more jewels and gowns and magical artifacts than she could count, and *power.* The power to achieve anything she wanted. The power to punish her enemies. The power to never again be told what to do.

In her many, many daydreams about this moment, she'd imagined herself laughing, singing, burning down cities, dancing wildly across the sky. But here it was at last, and instead she'd found this grand, saturated peace.

She had nothing left to fear. In the whole world. Nothing at all.

Vivienne rose and swept to the nearest window, her glossy mane of black feathers and Kalidah-fur robes shimmering around her.

There was plenty to see from her lair. Some windows showed the rocks and thistles of the Laughing Waste, others the floating boulders of Bobbing Canyon or the rippling waves of the Unnamed Prairies. This one looked out over snow-covered peaks, rainbows flickering in their waterfalls, and the forests below so green she could almost taste the richness of fir and pine.

The sky above was the pale blue of late afternoon, but banks of charcoal clouds were massing together in the west. Winter was coming. Soon the cold would sweep across Oz.

Already the winds were picking up around her lair, and

Vivienne watched as a gust buffeted a passing mustard bird, making it battle to stay aloft.

She smiled at its struggles, her red lacquered teeth gleaming. She might have nothing to fear anymore, but there were still potential annoyances to be dealt with—the staff and students of the School for Wicked Witches, for instance—and the bird's predicament reminded her of a particularly nasty spell in *Volatilium Gemmis.*

The calm inside Vivienne gave way to a giggle, then a laugh, then a cackle sharp as broken glass, filling her lair and echoing to the very top of the wide, unsuspecting sky.

2

THE BUMP IN THE NIGHT

Ava Heartstraw lay wide awake in her room at the top of Nettle Tower, feeling very, very anxious.

Night pressed against the windows, letting only faint wisps of starlight through to show the cozy double dorm room. Ava's side was plain and tidy as always; the other wore its usual string lights, dried herbs, stacks of books, and scrawled magical symbols, though the purple-blanketed bed was cold and empty.

Seven weeks had passed since Ava's frenemy and roommate, Tinabella Grouse, had been separated from the rest of the school following Vivienne Morderay's attack. The School for Wicked Witches had survived the crisis—after some chaos involving an ancient security system beneath Nettle Tower—and Ava and her friends Henry Buffle and Crow Backpatch had even emerged as heroes. But Tinabella, who'd tried to double-cross all of them right at the end, was in big, big trouble.

Thanks to her, Vivienne Morderay was more dangerous than ever, and while the teachers and Warden Pike were keeping the details of Vivienne's visit under wraps, the whole school had noticed the tension as they waited to see if and when she would attack again.

Ava stared into the dark, her brain buzzing like a sugared-up cactus wasp. She hadn't been sleeping well, not for weeks. She had good reasons. So many, in fact, that she'd organized them into a list.

First, there was Tinabella. Warden Pike had finally broken down under Ava's persistent questioning and told her that Tinabella was locked up somewhere in the sprawling fortress, that she was safe, that she was continuing with her lessons, and that she was receiving regular lectures about her behavior, attitude, and choices.

Ava could only imagine how furious that must be making her roommate. Tinabella would probably be pricklier than ever when she was released—which, according to Warden Pike, would be in just a few days. Ava's stomach lurched each time she thought of Tinabella's face the last time she'd seen her, the hurt and anger in her eyes. Their reunion was sure to be uncomfortable.

The second reason Ava couldn't sleep was Midwinter testing. Nettle's must-pass magic tests had seemed a long way off through the autumn, but with two weeks to go, Ava, Crow, and Henry were suddenly very behind on their studying. Ava's juggling was coming along okay, but she still couldn't hold a circle of protection against an astral attack, and her grasp on Azimoth's list of the top one hundred magical plants was appalling. Henry and Crow had similar problems, or worse, and Ava was just as worried for them as she was for herself as day by day their chance to catch up vanished.

Finally, there were the symbols on her hands. If there was a secret to the scars the Stinging Hammer had burned into Ava's palms, she hadn't found it yet. The Moldy Horse had called the shapes a *sigil* and told her they were probably something special to do with the Nettle Smith. Ava had daydreamed about fabulous new powers, of course, like the ones the Nettle Smith's treasures had briefly given her down in the Bitter Forge. But the longer she went without answers, the more doubts and worries began to creep in, especially since the scars kept randomly tingling.

All of that combined with the constant threat of another, possibly much worse Vivienne Morderay attack made it a wonder she was getting any sleep at all.

Things weren't *completely* bad, at least. She and the boys had finally finished their detention with the Yellow Brick Road bricks just a few days ago. Being allowed to use magic had made a massive difference, and her control over her water magic was better than ever.

Now if only she could start getting some rest at night, maybe she could get on top of things.

Ava tugged the blankets around her and rolled over, trying to will the heaviness of sleep into her limbs.

Bump!

Ava opened her eyes.

What was that . . . ?

Bump!

Ava sat up.

It was coming from the hall.

Bump-bump!

Something was outside her room, thudding against the door.

Once Ava might have pulled the covers over her head and waited until whatever it was went away. But she'd been through some adventures lately. She might still be a few months off from turning twelve, but she wasn't the same nervous kid who'd first arrived at Swickwit.

She jumped up, pulling on slippers the same deep green as her pajamas, and tiptoed across the floor, conjuring a tiny glowing ball.

Bump!

Ava took a deep breath, trying not to imagine what kind of cursed, carnivorous, hungry creatures might be making the noise.

She yanked open the door, flaring her light . . .

And found herself face-to-face with a large brown book hovering in midair.

The book gave a fluttering start, then spun on its spine, flapping away excitedly down the hall.

Ava blinked.

A flying book had not been on her list of possible nighttime visitors. At least it seemed safe, and probably worth investigating. Her curiosity was as wide awake as the rest of her now.

Ava tiptoed after the book, passing the rooms of her sleeping Nettle classmates. The door into the Round Room was standing open, so Ava sent her ball ahead to check that the coast was clear. The light showed the benches around the walls, the letters in the floor, and the lamps in their niches, same as ever. But as she stepped out of the hallway, she stopped, her heart somersaulting.

The Round Room was home to two portal doors, one that teleported Nettle students to a laboratory—which Ava had *still* never seen, thanks to her classmate Jadis—and one that led to the enormous Swickwit library. Both were kept magically locked outside of the students' free afternoon and evening hours.

But now the door to the library was standing open, and an enormous *something* waited on the other side, its glossy black eyes gazing right at Ava.

It had the shape of an upright, vaguely human beetle. Its dangling feet floated above the ground. The flying book fluttered helplessly between two of its six gnarled hands.

Ava gulped.

"Oh, thank goodies," rumbled the creature in a deep, resonant voice. "I wasn't certainty that would work. Come quickness, something terrible has happened to Tinabella!"

3

THE FIRST PROBLEM

"B-Burdock?" said Ava. "Is that you?"

The librarian of Swickwit beamed down at her, his rotting-meat stench drifting into the Round Room, the library stretching out dark and brooding behind him.

"It is! I am so sorrowful to have wakened you."

Ava increased the glow of her light a little more. Last time she'd seen Burdock, the school had been locked in Wicked Mode, and he'd appeared as a giant, adorable hedgehog. Talking to him in this shape was going to take some getting used to.

"Did you send that book to wake me up?" she asked.

"Indeedly!"

"But how? How are you even here? Warden Pike closed the loopholes on the portal doors himself."

"Ah, but all doors have two sidings!" Burdock bobbed a bow. "As the librarian, I can openify anything from the library side whenever I want."

"That's useful," Ava said. "But then why not just come in?"

"Because I cannot leavify the library."

"Oh, right. So, what's up with Tinabella? Have you seen her? Is she okay?"

Burdock raised two of his free hands. "I have not *seen* her, but we have been correspondencing regularly. Until yesterday, that is."

"Tell me everything," said Ava.

Burdock did.

Apparently, Tinabella was being kept someplace called the Punzell Tower, which had no stairs and could only be reached through a secret portal door in the library. Professor Mulch had been visiting every afternoon to give her lessons and homework so she wouldn't fall behind before Midwinter testing, and she had food and a bed and room to run around and everything, but it still sounded grim.

"So if you haven't seen her, have you two been talking through the door, or something?" Ava asked the librarian.

"Misfortunately, no. It is not an open portal like this one. The teachers can pass in and out, as can school supplies, but nothing else. Luckily, the warden has allowified Tinabella to continue checking out books—you know what a great reader she is. So she writes me notes requestifying certain topics, and I write notes back when I deliverate them. I deliverated the latest stack last morning, but when I woke up tonight, there were no returns waiting, and no note." Burdock fluttered his wing case nervously. "That has not happened before."

"And you want me to . . . what?"

"Pop your head through the portal and check on her. You should be ably to since you are not the prisoner. I cannot because it would be leavifying the library."

Ava bit her lip. "Will that be safe?"

"Certainty! Or I would not have asked. Please, Ava, I'm terribly worrified about her!"

Not sure what else she could do, Ava nodded.

"This way!"

It was strange to be back in the library at night, hurrying along in Burdock's wake between shadowy shelves and tables. Ava couldn't help thinking of her last moonlit trip among the books, when she and Henry and Crow had carried out their misguided but successful escape from the school. That felt like years ago now.

Burdock finally came to a halt at an enormous gold-framed painting of badgers playing tennis. Releasing the fluttering book, he took hold of the frame with all six arms and pulled. It slid smoothly sideways, revealing an arch of gleaming quicksilver.

"Normal-wise, Tinabella's book returns would be piled up right here," said Burdock. "But as you see, nothing."

Ava gave the portal a wary look. The rippling shiny surface made her feel a bit queasy.

"So . . . I just stick my head into that?" she asked.

"Indeedly."

"Won't Tinabella be asleep?"

"I expectate so. Please wake her, Ava. Something is wrong; I can sense it."

Bracing one arm on either side of the arch, Ava squeezed

her eyes shut, held her breath, and plunged her head into the silvery haze.

She'd traveled by unknown portal once before, when a secret grandfather clock had sent her to West Oz Witch Academy and back. That journey had made her feel like a coin being flipped. This portal felt like burying her head in a pile of very cold, very fuzzy blankets.

When her senses settled down, she opened her eyes.

She was gazing into a large, domed room. Starlight shone through a circle of balconied windows high above, below which a railed walkway spiraled and zigzagged up and down the wall. At floor level there was a bed, a desk, a wardrobe, and three squashy old sofas shoved together. The whole place was messy and disordered—one giant book in particular caught Ava's eye, sprawled on its back like it had been hurled across the floor—but that at least was reassuringly familiar. Tinabella had definitely made herself at home.

The girl in question lay fast asleep in the bed. Ava felt a complicated tumble of emotions at the sight of her friend's silver skin, black bob haircut, and permanent scowl.

This was about to get awkward.

"Psst," she hissed. "Tinabella."

Tinabella grumbled in her sleep.

"Tina-belllllla," she called, a little louder.

Nothing.

"Hey! WAKE UP!" Ava shouted.

Tinabella jolted upright and stared around, blinking. Her eyes found Ava, and she screamed.

Ava figured the sight of her disembodied head floating in the portal could explain that well enough. But it did not explain why Tinabella threw back the covers and shouted, "Two cups diced carrotmallow!"

"Um," Ava said. "What?"

Tinabella leapt out of bed, conjuring a ball of icy blue light.

"Sauté until golden," Tinabella said excitedly, running toward her. "Then add the crushed ironmint and a generous pinch of pickled paper!"

"Sure," said Ava. "How . . . are you?"

"Cool before serving!" Tinabella declared, throwing her arms around Ava's neck.

Well, trying to, anyway. Tinabella's hands bounced off empty air an inch from Ava's skin.

"Huh," said Ava, watching her try again. "Looks like you can't touch me while I'm part of the portal."

"Ugh! Bring five quarts green ant broth to a boil." Tinabella waved her arms, looking furious.

Ava cleared her throat. "I—Wow, this is weird. It seems like maybe you can't talk normally right now?"

Tinabella bugged out her eyes, giving a very sarcastic nod.

"Okay. That's rough. I'm not here to rescue you, by the way, in case you were hoping. Burdock got me up to check on you because you stopped returning your library books. He's worried."

"Puree the skraggle berries until they gelatinize," said Tinabella. She pointed accusingly at the big book lying open on the floor. "Scrape back into the pot and add the simmering lilies." She jabbed her finger again. "The simmering lilies!"

"Riiiight," said Ava. "Look, can you try to tell me what's going on some other way? Without words?"

A frustratingly slow round of miming followed, but in the end, Ava finally thought she understood what had happened.

"So you tried to escape by smuggling yourself out inside a library book," she said. "Which honestly sounds like a good idea. But your spell went wrong, and instead the book became part of you?"

Tinabella nodded, her expression equal parts exasperation and regret.

"And the book you chose was *1001 Savory Soups of Oz,* and so now you can only speak in soup recipes."

More nods from Tinabella.

Ava worked very hard not to laugh. It wasn't funny, of course.

But it kind of was.

There was an inquiring tap on her left shoulder, and Ava remembered Burdock, patiently waiting and unable to hear anything going on. She gave him a thumbs-up with one hand and asked for a couple more minutes with the other.

"Okay, I get that it was an accident," she said. "Only why didn't you write a note to Burdock asking for a counterspell or something?"

Tinabella snatched a crumpled piece of paper from the desk and held it up for Ava to see.

Ava read aloud, "'Blend until chunky, then add nine clear rose petals. Top with slimy banana seeds and serve.'" She glanced at her friend. "It happens when you write, too? Ouch. Why did you try to escape in the first place, though? There's only a few days till they let you out."

The look Tinabella gave her could have curdled milk.

"And wait," Ava went on as a new thought struck her. "What if you get in trouble for trying to escape? Professor Mulch will totally notice when she comes in for your lessons. What if Warden Pike finds out? What if he makes you stay in here longer? What if this makes everything worse?"

Tinabella flared out both hands in a *Trust me, I know!* gesture.

Somewhere at the back of her mind, Ava realized she was totally enjoying having Tinabella like this. It left her free to ask questions and come up with her own ideas on how to fix things.

There was another tap on her shoulder.

"I think I gotta go," she said to Tinabella. "I'll tell Burdock what happened. He'll probably know some way to fix you. I mean, he *is* in charge of all the school's books. If you're still stuck when Professor Mulch comes tomorrow, maybe just pretend to have a cold so you can't speak? And, um, hand cramps or something so you can't write?"

Tinabella nodded. The fight seemed to have drained out of her. "Simmer over a low heat for two hours," she said.

"Sure, exactly," said Ava. "Bye. Try to get some sleep."

Swapping one last sad smile with her friend, Ava tugged her head back through the portal.

"Well?" rumbled Burdock, clicking three sets of fingers together. "What happened? Is she wellness?"

Ava explained.

"Oh, that poor girl," Burdock said, drooping. "We must keep her out of troublement, but I doubt I'll find a fix in what's left of tonight. What a mighty messness for her to make!"

"She does like being in charge and doing exactly what she wants," Ava pointed out. "Being locked away like this is probably super hard on her."

Burdock nodded. "Truthity. It has been hard. Tinabella acts tough, but this world can be very stormy to live in, and we all need the help and comforter of our peers."

"Is there anything I can do to help?"

"You already have." One craggy beetle hand patted her on the shoulder. "I will come knocking again at nightfall tomorrow, hopefully with the counterspell. You are an excellence friend to us both."

Five minutes later Ava was back in her bed in Nettle

Tower, snuggling under the covers and trying to untangle her feelings.

It had been good to see Tinabella, even with the soup problem. It felt like reaching the end of a long dream, the final chapter in the adventure of the Nettle Smith and Vivienne's attack. If they could cure Tinabella and keep her out of trouble for a few more days, everything would more or less go back to normal.

Well, as normal as anything ever got around here. How life would be once Tinabella moved back in and rejoined the class was an open question, but Ava was ready for it. Strained friendship or not, she *needed* Tinabella to be okay.

Because Ava had been tempted, too.

She'd heard the call of Vivienne Morderay's power loud and clear. She'd felt that craving for glory. She'd even briefly considered running away to become the wicked witch's apprentice herself.

She was more like Tinabella than anyone knew.

That meant she had to find a way to help her keep out of trouble. It was one more thing to add to her list of worries, but she should be able to manage it.

Just so long as absolutely nothing else went wrong at Swickwit.

4
THE COUNTDOWN CLOCK

Ava woke late the next morning. Yawning, she washed, dressed, and hurried into the Round Room, which hummed with her Nettle classmates finishing breakfast.

Most of them, anyway. Wolfgang Hex and Dorian Cob were missing, since Professor Mulch had made good on her threat from the start of the year and turned them both into desks for being tardy to class for the second time.

One other change caught Ava's eye as she grabbed cereal and a plorange yogurt: The enormous countdown clock Professor Mulch had conjured beside the classroom door now shone with an ominous, glowing 13. Less than two weeks to go until Midwinter testing.

Ava dropped onto her usual bench beside Henry and Crow.

"Morning," Henry said.

"Hi hi," said Crow around a mouthful of buttermint toast.

"Hey!" Ava gestured them close, dropping her voice to a whisper. "You will not *believe* what happened last night. I talked to Tinabella!"

Briefly, she recounted her midnight trek.

"Whoa!" said Crow. "That's so cool she can talk in soupish

now! I wonder if that means she can communicate with it."

"I really hope Burdock fixes her before she gets in worse trouble," Henry murmured.

"'Cause that would make mealtimes amazing," continued Crow. "Maybe soup's been trying to communicate with us for centuries, and Tinabella will be the first person to find out!"

Ava grinned. "I think she's just speaking in recipes. Not some secret soup language."

"Aw, too bad. We could have called her the Soup-unicator."

"Do you think we should try to help?" asked Henry. "We could look up counterspells after lunch. Maybe leave a note for Burdock if we find anything?"

"'At's a 'reat idea," Ava said, shoveling down her cereal.

"Or how about the Soup Whisperer?" said Crow.

"I was hoping to work on my next piece for poetry club today," Henry said, going a little pink around the ears. "But this is more important."

"Ooh! Soup Whooper!" Crow clapped his hands. "That's it. That has to be it."

Ava was opening her mouth to explain again about Tinabella and the cookbook when the classroom door flew open and a booming call of "Enter! Class is now in session!" rolled through the room.

Scarfing down the last of her breakfast, she grabbed her spell book and filed inside with the rest.

* * *

Heavy winter rain had been hammering Oz for most of the past week, but the huge window shone that morning with pale sunlight glowing through the fog off the boiling lake. Ava gave the slithering walls a pat on the way to her seat, something she did now every time she entered the classroom. She and those roots had shared some real adventures. They were practically old friends.

Professor Mulch waited up front by the rolling blackboard, barely as tall as the students and wearing her usual Nettle-green robes. Her antlers were medium-sized today and decorated with looping black and silver ribbons that swung gently on their own.

"Seats!" she bellowed as they all hurried to their places. Opal Havnor tripped over Branwen and had to do a bounce charm to avoid a bad crash. When everyone was finally seated, the professor narrowed her eyes.

"Does everyone believe me now about the consequences of being late to class?" she asked.

They all nodded, shooting looks at the extra empty desks that were Wolfgang and Dorian.

"And we all agree punctuality is *extremely important*? Especially when the clock shows only thirteen days until your Midwinter testing?"

Everyone nodded some more.

"Good!"

Professor Mulch waved a hand, and the two desks rocked,

shuddered, and transformed into their missing classmates, both looking rumpled and extremely self-conscious.

"Sit!" ordered Professor Mulch. Wolfgang and Dorian sat. "Right, here's what we're doing this morning!" She slapped the blackboard, and a complicated tangle of symbols appeared across it. "We'll start by reviewing quick-cast circles of protection. Some of you are proficient, but others are still shaky, and quite apart from the fact that they will definitely be on the Midwinter test, I want to know all my students are able to call on a basic defense against any, well, *dangers* that might arise."

Ava shared a glance with Henry and Crow. Apart from Jonsi, the rest of the class had no idea Vivienne Morderay had attacked them that autumn, or that she was more powerful than ever and almost certain to strike again. Professor Mulch knew, though, and she was clearly worried.

Jonsi had never brought up Vivienne's visit, not once in all the weeks since, leaving Ava to wonder if the dreamy, moody boy had even noticed the grand adventure he'd been a part of.

Carmelie raised a hand. "Can't we review dark rainbows instead?" she asked. "I mean, if some people here are already good enough at circles . . ."

She left the question hanging in the air, and Ava knew why: Carmelie was top of the class in dark rainbows, and very nearly the worst at quick-cast anything.

Professor Mulch shook her head. "No, Miss Wright, we cannot." One of the ribbons in her antlers unfurled, dangling into her eyes. She waved it back into place. "And after teaching for ninety-seven years"—she paused while the class broke into applause—"I know exactly what game you're playing. There is never a good time to show off, squidgelings, but these thirteen days are the absolute worst time to do it!"

Carmelie's rosy cheeks flushed a deeper pink, but she kept her chin up. Ava quirked a tiny smile. Carmelie had created plenty of trouble for her since her arrival at Swickwit, and they were definitely a long way from friends, but Ava still had to admire the girl sometimes. She had confidence to spare, and she was always willing to ask for exactly what she wanted.

"This is the time to dig in, to push!" Professor Mulch shouted, her eyes burning as she surveyed the class. "That clock in the Round Room is going to say *ten* before you can blink, then *seven*, then *five*. Think of who you want to be when it says *one*!"

The antler ribbon unfurled again, this time joined by several others. Professor Mulch shot a glance out the window, a line appearing between her eyebrows as she flicked them back to their places.

"None of which," she continued, "is served by tinkering where you are already strong. Tell me, my witchikins, why do I keep bringing up your many, many weaknesses?" She stabbed a finger at Matthew. "Mr. Avalon!"

Matthew jumped. "Um, to make us feel bad?"

Professor Mulch chortled. "Wrong! Miss Frost?"

"Because your teachers were mean to you when you were a kid?"

"No! Miss Aspic?"

"To keep us from getting conceited?"

"Ha! Extra wrong, and no! I focus on your weaknesses because they are signposts to where you can make the most *progress*. Where you can experience the joy of explosive growth. Every weakness is an opportunity! A chance to level up fast!"

Professor Mulch was literally glowing, her words booming out like thunder and her eyes fixing each student in their seat as she strode back and forth across the classroom.

"Your weaknesses are *treasure*! And I demand you seize every last bit of it! Pull each drop of potential out of this precious place and time! I want you to shock me and Warden Pike and the entire school with how much magic you can learn. I know you are capable of it! And do you know why?"

The class, rapt and staring, waited breathlessly for the answer.

But Professor Mulch never got to tell them, because at that moment every ribbon around her antlers whipped upward, straining to attention like swords pointing to the sky, and the whole world went *FWOOM*.

5
A SECOND PROBLEM

Ava was five years old when she saw her first winter sandstorm sweep over her home on the edge of the Impassable Desert.

She remembered it in flashes: the sickly orange sky, the crack in her mother's voice shouting her twelve children inside, the hissing roar hammering the walls of their little house, the darkness, the eerie silence after, the days of sweeping to uncover the buried brick moss fields.

It all raced through her mind again as an enormous *something* touched down outside the school. Something that shook the walls of Swickwit, rattling the students out of their desks and filling the air with a booming, thrumming, crackling howl that went on and on and on.

Then, all at once, the floor beneath them stilled, the familiar fog outside vanished, and muddy amber light flooded the classroom.

Professor Mulch rushed to the window. Everyone followed.

Squeezing in beside their professor, Ava, Crow, and Henry gazed out at a transformed world.

The hills of broken glass were gone, sucked up like dead

leaves into a massive, brooding wall of wind spinning just beyond the boiling lake and towering as high as they could see into the sky.

It was as though some unthinkable creature had swallowed the school whole, lake and island and all.

"What is it?" cried Beryl.

"It's a cyclone!" shouted Margo.

"No, a tempest!" hollered Dorian.

"It must be a curse!" Opal gasped.

"Who would curse Swickwit?" said Wolfgang.

"Lots of people!" Branwen snapped.

"But who could do *this*?!" demanded Carmelie.

"Vivienne Morderay," answered Jonsi.

Ava almost got an antler in the eye as every head turned.

Jonsi stood at the far end of the window, one hand resting on the glass, his huge gray eyes gleaming in the strange light.

"Vivienne Morderay?!" said Carmelie. "What in Oz does she have to do with our school?"

"And how would you know?" demanded Matthew.

Jonsi gave a slow blink. "I recognize her magic. There's a big thread of it running through the wind." He pointed. "Just there."

There was a heartbeat of silence while the whole class absorbed the idea that Jonsi could *see* magic, then the hubbub began.

"How could *you* recognize—"

"Is he right, Professor? Is it Vivienne?"

"—mean we're in danger?"

"She's *actually* wicked!"

"What if it comes closer?"

"What if it eats the school?"

Ava had a front-row seat to the expression on her wizened teacher's face, and what she saw made her blood freeze over: Professor Mulch looked scared.

"D-don't worry," Ava called, adding her voice to the noise. "Even if it is Vivienne Morderay, Warden Pike will stop her!"

Murmurs of agreement rose from the class, until another voice cut them off.

"Warden Pike," Professor Mulch said, "is not here."

"Where is he?" asked Opal.

"Away."

Crow cleared his throat. "He can, uh, get back, though, right?"

"Through this?" Professor Mulch shook her antlers. "I strongly doubt it."

"That sounds like . . . maybe a problem?" said Henry.

The class went silent. The wind roared.

Professor Mulch's face changed again. She drew herself up.

"Yes, it is," she said. "It is a disruption during a crucial point in your education, and I will not have it." Her voice returned to full strength. "Stand back, little doomcakes!"

The students did as they were told, bumping into one another and their desks as Professor Mulch placed both palms against the glass, chanting softly, and the window disappeared.

The howl of the windstorm swept over them all, a tooth-thrumming rumble blended with the endless tinkling of shattered glass.

The air smelled of lightning. It made the back of Ava's neck prickle.

"Stay," Professor Mulch ordered, her eyes on the storm and her words landing heavy as dropped stones in the terrified classroom, "here."

And spreading her arms wide, she threw herself into the sky.

6

A THIRD PROBLEM

The whole class rushed back to the missing window. Ava had to grab Henry to stop him from being knocked through by the kids behind.

Everyone gazed out at Professor Mulch soaring majestically over the towers and rooftops of Swickwit, her green robes flapping around her.

"I can't wait till I can fly," sighed Beryl. "How cool will it be to say, *Hey, gravity! I defy you!*"

"Anyone think she can stop the storm?" Crow asked.

"I bet she can," said Margo.

"Bet she can't," said Wolfgang.

"She's gonna try, though," Opal cried. "Look!"

They all did, and saw the other teachers flying up to meet Professor Mulch: Professor Dust from Cauldron, with her copper robes and six eyes, and Cobweb's Professor Nightshade wrapped in gray, her gold hands shining in the strange light.

The Nettle students leaned out, craning their necks to see the teachers come together in the air, gesturing and shouting. All three crackled with power, and Ava found herself agreeing with Beryl: She couldn't wait until she was older and came into her full strength. She'd never really thought about what she might be like as a grown-up before; it seemed so far-off it was like another world. But she would get there someday, she supposed, and when she did, she hoped she was something like her teachers.

With maybe, whispered a voice inside her, *a bit of Vivienne Morderay's style thrown in.*

The witches high above came to some agreement, and the shouting ended as they joined hands.

"They're trying something!" yelled Dorian.

A gleaming purple light appeared between the teachers, so deep it was almost black. It splintered into arcing threads, forming a lattice from hand to hand, and the teachers flew apart, pulling the light into a wide triangular web.

"Hey, careful!" said Branwen, grabbing Jadis's robes as she leaned out over the dizzying drop.

"I can't see anymore!" Jadis complained.

"Same," said Crow. "Why don't we all climb up on the roof? It'll be easy with the roots, and we'll have the best view in Swickwit!"

The class's reactions to this suggestion ranged from terror (Henry) to glee (Margo), but after a brief debate everyone agreed it would be worth the risk to see exactly what was going on.

Ava was fascinated by the different ways her classmates tackled the climb. She didn't think any of them had ever scaled living roots hundreds of feet off the ground before, but some, like Dorian and Beryl, scampered up as though there were nothing to it. Wolfgang went slowly and cautiously, his tongue between his teeth. Carmelie kept up a running commentary about how gross the writhing roots were, holding her head back so they wouldn't touch her hair. It took both Ava and Crow to help Henry over the window ledge, boosting and reassuring with a constant stream of encouragements as they made their way up together.

At last they were all standing safe and sound on the gently sloping roof of Nettle Tower.

A giddy exhilaration surged through the group as they took in their surroundings, partly from the fact they were somewhere they were definitely not supposed to be, and partly because the view awaiting them was utterly terrifying.

The panorama of Swickwit rooftops and towers that had captivated Ava, Crow, and Henry on their last visit was completely irrelevant now.

The sky itself was gone.

The school stretched out around them, then the boiling lake, then nothing but the wall of wind, rising in an unimaginable funnel high, high overhead before finally fusing into a seething clot of darkness.

Ava gaped, her head craned back as far as it would go, then quickly sat down like many of her classmates, not trusting her balance under that dizzying vortex.

Dim sunlight glittered off the flying glass. The roar of the maelstrom filled the world. But the air inside the storm was deathly still; not even a wisp of a breeze ran across the rooftops of the school.

Amid it all, the teachers' triangle of magic was still growing, the searing purple becoming more intense until they finally came to a halt, each hovering directly beside the wall of air. Their web covered the whole view now, crackling with sparks, letting off an ominous metallic pinging. Ava had never seen magic like it.

"Ooh, this is gonna be good!" someone said.

"Go Professor Mulch!"

"Woo!"

Ava's eyes darted from teacher to teacher as they all made an identical complicated gesture with their hands. There was a fizzing sound, a pause, then bolts of black lightning arced from every side of the web directly into the storm.

With a groan, the wall of air and dirt and glass stopped spinning.

The class erupted in cheers, but they only got a few moments of relief before the funnel lurched, stuttered, and started up again.

Ava couldn't quite follow everything that happened next, but from one blink to the next the spell web was torn asunder, sending the purple threads flailing while a rain of sparks cascaded onto the school below.

The professors shouted in unison, the beginning of a

counterspell, maybe, or a shield, but the lashing remnants were already being drawn into the maelstrom, and in another blink all three had been wrapped up from head to toe and dragged along with them.

The last fragments of the web winked out as the Nettle students, alone on their rooftop in the center of Swickwit, stared at the storm that had just swallowed the only grown-ups left in the fortress.

"Well," said Margo after a long, horrified moment. "That's definitely a problem."

7

THE CRISIS

"What do we do?!"

"Oh no, oh no, oh no!"

"Help!"

All the Nettle students were on their feet, staring in horror at the storm.

"Look!" shouted Wolfgang, pointing. "You can still see them!"

Ava followed his finger in time to see a clot of copper robes whiz by on the wind, followed by a lump of green that had to be Professor Mulch and a gray shadow that must be Professor Nightshade. The teachers had become part of the storm, zooming around and around amid the dirt and fog and broken glass.

"I hope they're not getting sliced to pieces," moaned Opal.

"Seriously!" said Ava. She and Crow hurried across the roof to join Henry, who was clinging with both hands to the spike at the center.

"Someone do something!" Carmelie shouted. "Throw a rope!"

Multiple students pointed out the lack of ropes, and the question of how to find some quickly turned into an argument.

"Wait! Ava!" said Crow. "What about water? Could you pull them out using water from the lake?"

Ava felt a thrill run through her. The day was in total upheaval—only twenty minutes ago they'd been starting class!—but life at Swickwit had been getting downright predictable since Vivienne Morderay's departure. The chance to be part of something important again felt wonderful, even if it was a crisis. And after all, teacher rescues *were* one of her specialties.

"Crow, that's brilliant!" she said. "I'll try."

"W-won't the boiling water hurt them?" asked Henry.

Ava waved the problem away. "It'll be worth it if it gets them out of that storm. Besides, they're teachers; they'll be able to heal a few burns!"

With her classmates busy bickering, Ava strode to the edge of the roof and gazed out, wishing there were a breeze to blow dramatically through her hair as she opened to her water magic and connected with the lake below.

"Whoa!" cried Branwen when Ava's writhing rope of water climbed into view. More sounds of surprise came from all around her, but she was too busy concentrating to respond.

Her classmates quieted, and she could feel their eyes on her as she coiled the end of the water into a loop, guiding it up beside the storm, level with the teachers. Fighting the wind's pull, she waited . . . and waited . . . savoring her moment as the center of attention . . .

"Now!" someone yelled, and Ava, startled, slammed half her water directly into the wind.

"WHOAOAOAOO!"

Instantly, she was violently dizzy. The world tilted and the stormy sky went sideways as, disoriented, she took one wild, lunging step . . . and fell off the roof.

Everyone gasped.

Ava plummeted, losing her hold on the remaining water, sending the column crashing back into the lake.

Her classmates' shouts barely had time to finish, though, before one of the tower's nettle roots slashed across the distance and caught her by the ankle in midair.

The next thing she knew, she was being safely deposited, shaking like a baby moss mouse, onto the roof amid her classmates.

"Ava!"

"Holy hicklebrick!"

"—*such* a show-off."

"How did the roots do that?"

"Are you okay?!"

Henry and Crow crowded over her, patting her back.

"Ugh, I am never trying that again," Ava said, when she could speak. "It felt like the storm was inside my head! Thank Oz for those roots. But who scared me by shouting 'Now'?"

"Me." Beryl raised a hand. "What? You were taking forever."

"And it didn't work, anyway," said Carmelie. "We need an actual plan. Or, you know, some real help. Where are all the older students?"

As though she'd summoned them, a dozen teenagers in black suddenly appeared between the forest of towers.

"Ohh," said Beryl. "That's why they call it Broom."

Several people laughed, but Ava wasn't one of them. She'd never questioned the names of their class levels—Nettle, Cobweb, Cauldron, Broom—but the sight of the school's oldest students rising in the air on ragged broomsticks made her wonder if she'd ever paid attention to anything at all.

The Broom students zoomed directly over Nettle Tower, but even in this crisis the old rule stuck, and none of them so much as glanced at the young crowd gawking from the roof. Ava heard a wild-haired girl at the front shouting something as they passed.

"Hey, neat," said Jonsi.

Ava jumped, surprised at the rare reaction from the quiet boy.

"What's neat?"

"They're all sending magic to that girl." Jonsi pointed. "I think maybe she's leading a group spell."

Everyone watched as the twelve flying teenagers floated to a stop near the wall of wind. Forming a rough circle, they began chanting, and a frosty blue light appeared around the wild-haired girl, reminding Ava of the halo she sometimes saw ringing the moon on winter nights in the desert.

The girl lifted her arms, and the glow spread, surrounding her companions. Then all their arms were waving, the light shifting back and forth, pulsing and growing as they swayed side to side.

"Huh," said Jonsi.

"What is it?" asked Ava. "What are they doing now?"

"I don't know. But it's pretty complicated."

With a shout the Broom students broke their circle, joining hands to form a glowing chain. Lining the rest of her classmates up behind her, the lead girl raised her free hand and pushed their shimmering blue creation directly into the wind.

"NO!"

The bellow rang over the towers of Swickwit, startling a flock of rotting pigeons who had settled on a nearby rooftop.

Every Nettle head turned as Gern the gargoyle appeared, belting up from the school below, his stone wings pummeling the air.

"Stop!" he shouted as he flew. "'S too dangerous!"

A few Broom students turned to look, but their leader kept pressing forward. Just as the gargoyle reached for the nearest teenager, her spell made contact.

A furious, silent blast washed over them all as the blue glow exploded, disappearing on the wind with the Broom students, still holding hands and looking very surprised, tumbling in after it.

Gern twisted out of danger at the last second, roaring in frustration as he flew in a long, banking arc. Then he spotted the Nettle kids.

"Oi!"

With another curl of his wings, he was plummeting toward them.

Gern landed with a crashing thud, his enormous stone wolf-man-bat body leaving deep claw marks on the tiles. The class gaped, and Dorian and Matthew had to jump out of the way as he strode directly for Ava, Crow, and Henry, his face furious.

"All right, you three," he barked. "What in the name o' Lurline 'ave yeh done now?!"

8

WARDEN PIKE

The field mouse in the second-to-last teapot balanced on the back of the Great Lacquered Tortoise was being very difficult.

Warden Threnody Pike shifted impatiently on the wet grass. His mission to find out what Vivienne Morderay might be planning had so far been utterly unsuccessful. He hadn't even tracked down her secret hideout, even though everyone knew it was somewhere in North Oz. It was very troubling.

True, Vivienne was dangerously strong now—which was why he'd risked leaving the school to spy on her—and likely protecting herself in new and powerful ways. It still ate at him to have failed so completely.

He'd been flying back to Swickwit, weary and worried, when he'd spotted the Great Lacquered Tortoise trundling through the grasslands not far from the school. He'd groaned at the sight of it, but a chance was a chance, and he'd slipped reluctantly out of the sky to land beside it.

Fifteen deeply frustrating minutes later, he was almost getting somewhere.

The tortoise clacked its beak, and Pike hastily fed it another gold coin, giving the field mouse his best attempt at a winning smile.

"Sir Nibbles," he said as the cold wind stung the back of his neck, "I have given you two rubies and a piece of cheese. I have sung the Song of Respectful Squeaking. I have stood on my head and wished I had whiskers in all nine mouse dialects. Will you please now grant my request and tell me where Vivienne Morderay is?"

Sir Nibbles looked up from his cheese, crumbs smeared across his velvet tunic.

"Possibilly," he squeaked. "It dependibillys on one final test."

Pike let out a sigh.

Sir Nibbles drew himself up, banging his gold helmet on the lid of his teapot. "I did not have to answer your knock, you know! Plentibilly of Oracles would ignore a witch with your reputation!" He straightened his emerald-rimmed glasses. "However, I happenibilly to be in a charitibilly mood. I will tell you where Vivibillyenne Morderay is in exchange for—"

FWOOM.

China rattled as the tortoise disappeared into its shell and Sir Nibbles vanished inside the teapot. Warden Pike jumped to his feet, turning toward the noise that had swept over the grasslands like the end of the world.

Something dark and massive was blotting out the horizon, filling the sky . . . in the direction of Swickwit.

Without warning, every alarm and protection spell Warden Pike had built between himself and the school went off at once.

A heartbeat later, he was in the air.

"Come back!" squeaked Sir Nibbles, poking his head out of his teapot. "It's too dangerbillyous! And I was onbilly going to ask for more cheddar and a diamond toothpick! I'll tell you! Come back!"

Warden Pike did not go back. All that mattered now was his school and the students within it.

Without thinking he shifted into a hawk, flying as only a bird of prey could, burning through the wind.

Below him his raptor eyes saw the small creatures of the grasslands stumbling and running, crawling up from their holes and homes, peering in shock at the strange new landmark.

Fear drove him forward, the world blurring as the thing on the horizon grew closer until it became a swirling wall filling his vision, and he dropped to the ground in his own shape, panting.

Silencing the alarm spells clanging within him, he took stock.

A raging storm had surrounded his school, its monstrous funnel churning and spinning just outside the wards.

"Clever," he muttered, leaning back to gaze up, up, up. The weak winter sun set off a glittering rainbow within the wind, and Warden Pike felt a pang of loss for his beautiful glass hills.

But what *was* this? Vivienne had conjured it—that was clear. This was the blow he'd been waiting for, the hammer of her pride and anger coming down at last. But what spell could make a storm this . . . grand?

Pike reached out with senses acquired through more years of magic than anyone in Oz suspected, probing. For a moment his inner eye was dazzled, then the threads began to fall into patterns. What he saw chilled his blood: perpetual motion, nasty time enchantments, whirlpools, vertigo, the void.

His focus broke as something powerful suddenly whipped past—powerful and alive. He scrabbled after it, barely registering one of his teachers before there was another, and another, followed by a linked line of lesser strength that had to be his poor Broom students.

Rage forged of pure terror filled Warden Pike, and he stretched his magical senses as far as he could to discover the fate of these people he was supposed to be protecting.

To his shock and relief, they appeared to be whole, unharmed, and . . . asleep. There were sleep spells woven through the time enchantments, the heavy, spinning-wheel kind that could last a thousand years or more. Peering closer, Pike saw the storm was not just an attack, but a cage. Those trapped in it were immobilized, like pieces taken off a game board, but not destroyed. For now, at least, they were safe.

A memory tugged at him, then another, and a grim recognition began assembling itself in his mind.

He tried one final test, knitting his fingers together and whispering an old raven charm through them. If the charm worked, he should be able to speak mind to mind with whoever in the castle was closest, if only for a moment.

The counterspell struck like lightning, sending him staggering back, his teeth aching. Raising a hand, he stared at his fingernails, now a sickly, chalky white.

Sour dread filled Warden Pike's stomach. His fears were confirmed.

Vivienne had called down Dorothy's Gale upon Swickwit.

It had been nearly two hundred years since this disaster had darkened the skies of Oz, and it had taken the Witch Council putting forth all its strength to banish it and the witch who'd cast it.

In the strangest way, Warden Pike was almost proud of Vivienne. It was an astonishing feat. A monumental piece of magic.

But he had to admit that he was scared.

His teachers were caught in that storm. His oldest, best-trained students were caught, too. He himself was trapped outside with no way in and no way to stop it. And scores of inexperienced, excitable, varyingly wicked young witches were now all alone in the fortress.

Well, apart from Gern.

A corner of Pike's mouth gave the faintest twitch. He hoped the gargoyle was up for a challenge.

As for him, this was beyond his power. Only the Witch Council could handle something like this. He despised dealing with them, but he had a duty to his students, his staff, and the school. Against that, his pride counted for nothing.

So, it was off to see the popular witches.

He returned to the air, a great crested crane this time, ready for the longer flight to the Witch Council Hall. His white wings held the wind as he circled, taking one last look at the storm, thinking of his students.

How long would he be gone? How long would it take the Council to defeat the storm . . . and hopefully Vivienne along with it? How long would his kids have to fend for themselves?

He could not smile as a bird, but he felt a spark of wild humor in his feathery chest as he considered those students still at large within the school.

Whatever happened, he knew young Ava Heartstraw would likely find some way to get involved. And under these conditions she would either save the day . . . or destroy his school once and for all.

9

THE TERRIBLE SITUATION

"Wh-what?" said Henry.

"Huh?" said Crow.

"It wasn't us!" insisted Ava.

"Oh, very likely!" Gern glared down at the three of them, and Ava realized she'd never seen him truly angry before. Or maybe truly scared. Either way it was alarming. "Whenever anythin's gone weird this year, you three are always par' of it! Now, what 'ave yeh done?"

Ava was saved from having to answer by her classmates.

"You seriously think *they* could do this?" scoffed Carmelie, gesturing dramatically overhead.

"Theirs would be more like a slime storm," Beryl said. "A small, boring one."

"Jonsi says it was Vivienne Morderay," said Jadis. "Isn't that wild?"

Gern's head whipped around to the gloomy boy.

"An' 'ow would you know tha'?" he demanded, his stone eyes wide.

Jonsi's shoulders rose and fell. "I can see it. It looks the same as the last time I saw it."

Gern's eyes somehow became even wider. "Yeh've got spell-sight?!"

"Maybe? I can see magic, if that's what you mean. Everyone's looks different."

Gern let out a sandy whistle. "Scrape my gravel. I've been Guardian 'ere for a hundred an' seventy-two years, an'—"

He cut off as the class broke into a loud round of applause.

"Er, thanks? I was sayin' I've never seen a group in Nettle as gifted an' troublesome as yours."

The class exchanged glances.

"Anyway," Gern growled, gazing out over their heads. "Least this storm don't seem to be really dangerous 'less you go near it."

"What do you think is happening to everyone who got dragged inside?" Matthew asked.

Gern looked grave. "Nothin' we can do but 'ope they're okay."

Crow raised a hand. "Where've you been, Gern? Why weren't you here when the teachers were trying their big web spell?"

"I was followin' orders! With Warden Pike out o' the castle, Professor Dust an' Professor Nightshade summoned me soon as the storm landed an' put me in charge of all their Cobweb an' Cauldron kids." He waved a hand at the school below. Ava craned her neck and saw crowds of older students in gray and copper robes filling the courtyards and stairs, milling around and gazing at the storm in horror.

"Shame they di'n't include the Broom students," Gern went on. "Might've been able t' stop them doin' such a foolish thing."

Ava's heart twinged at the heavy responsibility in his voice. "So, you're in charge of the whole school now?" she asked.

"Basic'ly," said Gern. "An' that's a lot o' rules an' students to keep organized." He glanced around. "None of you lot should be up 'ere fer a start. 'Ow'd that 'appen?"

Opal explained about Professor Mulch removing the window and their climb up the roots for a better view.

"Well, climb back in an' stay there, please. This roof's 'credibly dangerous."

"No, it's not!" declared Dorian, and without any warning he skipped to the edge and threw himself off.

Gern growled in alarm, but just like before, a long tendril of the Nettle Tower roots whipped out, snagging Dorian around the middle and dumping him back beside them.

"See?" he said, grinning. "Totally safe. Is that cool?"

"We can all show you if you want," offered Beryl.

"No!" Gern held up one giant hand. "Heavin' pyrite, don't think me deposits could take it."

"Well, you cannot expect us not to come up here," said Margo, her precise accent making her sound perfectly reasonable. "We are kids, you know. We have to explore."

Carmelie nodded. “Plus we don’t know how to magic up a new window, anyway.”

“Fine, fine!” Gern looked frazzled. “All right, let’s go over th’ whole terrible situation. Seein’ as I’m the only staff left, I don’t dare try me magic against the storm. Tha’ means our only ’ope is Warden Pike fixin’ things from the outside.” He sighed. “I’ll wrangle the Cobweb an’ Cauldron kids till then, but there’s scores o’ them, and I can’t be everywhere at once. So do you lot think you can look after yerselves fer a bit?”

Everyone started talking at once.

“Listen,” Gern growled over the noise. “You’ve got your own tower, an’ there’s only fourteen of yeh to start with!” He squinted around. “Wait, yeh are all ’ere, right? No one wandered off?”

All at once, Ava remembered.

“Tinabella!” she shrieked. “We have to rescue her!”

“Rescue?” said Branwen. “I thought she was in detention or whatever.”

“She is!” Ava said. “But with the teachers stuck in the storm, she’ll be all alone. Please, Gern? Warden Pike was going to let her out of Punzell Tower in a few days, anyway.”

Gern narrowed his eyes. “How d’ you know where she’s bein’ kept?”

Figuring this was no time to be piling on secrets, Ava explained about Burdock’s visit.

The gargoyle shook his head. "You do get into everythin' 'round here, Ava. It's uncanny."

"Thanks," said Ava, her emotions spinning. "But can we go now, please? Like you said, we should all be together, and—"

Gern cut her off. "I'll get Tinabella. No, jus' me. It'll be quicker on me own. You all sit tight an' please don't go throwin' yerselves off the roof anymore. Them roots may run out of patience."

Ava's mouth was already open to argue, but in a clatter of wings and claws, the grumbling gargoyle heaved up into the sky and took off across the school.

The moment he was gone, Ava, Henry, and Crow found themselves surrounded.

"Okay, how do you know Gern so well?" Dorian demanded. "I haven't talked to him since the Wicked Wagon."

"And why would he think you were behind the storm?" Branwen asked.

Wolfgang crossed his arms. "We know there's something up with you three. We've known for a while. So spill!"

Ava and the boys looked at one another. They weren't really supposed to tell the other students what had happened seven weeks ago, but no one had made them *promise* not to. And it did seem to be the time for sharing secrets.

Briefly, Ava related Vivienne's attack, the strange consequences of Wicked Mode, and the ancient Nettle defense system. She did her best to skim over her major role in saving the school and downplay the fact that Tinabella had tried to betray them all, but she didn't have to try too hard: Her classmates were more concerned about themselves.

"I was a giant cookie?!" shouted Carmelie.

"Better than a singing juggling ball like us!" countered Margo.

"I wish I could remember it," Matthew said.

"Okay, fine," said Wolfgang, facing Ava. "That explains some stuff, but not everything. What about earlier in the year? Were you three *really* lost in a hidden slime dimension?"

Henry gave a tiny squeak, and Crow shot Ava an unhelpfully guilty look.

She opened her mouth, wondering how convincingly she could lie with everyone watching—they actually had promised not to share *that* story—but she was saved by the sudden return of Gern.

Margo began the applause as the gargoyle swooped in for a landing, and soon everyone joined in.

They surged around Tinabella as she slid to the ground, an enormous book clutched in her arms. Jadis and Carmelie patted her shoulders while Beryl gave her an awkward hug, all of them asking how she was, where she'd been, if it was good to be back.

"Boil until the ostridon broth is reduced by half," Tinabella said over the noise.

The class went quiet, and Ava gasped, remembering a

fairly important detail she'd forgotten to mention earlier.

"Um, what?" said Dorian.

"Half a teaspoon powdered glueberry," replied Tinabella. "Divide into bowls and serve."

"Okay, seriously?" Carmelie threw her hands in the air. "This is getting ridiculous. What's going on *now*?"

10

ONE THING FIXED

"I'd like ter know that, too," said Gern. "Ava? Wot's wrong with Tinabella?"

Trapped under the whole class's attention once more, Ava explained about Tinabella's escape attempt and the accidental soup book merger.

"But Burdock thinks he can track down a counterspell or something," she finished. "He said he'll bring it by tonight."

Gern dragged one huge stone hand down his face.

"Tha' 'splains why she wouldn't leave tha' book behind. Seriously, you lot are jus' plain trouble." He turned to Tinabella. "Yer back now, at least. I trust ol' Burdy to get the job done curin' yeh, an' this lot'll fill yeh in abou' the storm. Think you'll be all right after that?"

Tinabella, still clutching the book to her chest, shrugged. "Heat the mashroot cream until steaming," she said.

Gern nodded. "Let's 'ope tha's good. Now then"—he raised his voice—"gather roun' an' listen up!"

He looked reassuringly strong, Ava thought, framed against the storm, his stone wings spread wide. She realized she was feeling close to overwhelmed. So much had happened in the last twelve hours, and was still happening. So much that had been stable and dependable in her world was suddenly up in the air—literally. It was a relief having the gargoyle there with them.

"I've got to go sor' out the Cobweb an' Cauldron kids now," declared Gern. "So I'll be leaving yeh on yer own."

Ava's heart dropped.

"Yer to stay t'gether as much as possible till Warden Pike fixes things," Gern went on. "No, no interruptin'! He will, an' soon. Yer job till then's to look after yerselves an' each other. I'll check back at the end of class ev'ry day to see 'ow yer gettin' on with yer studies."

That got a reaction.

"Wait, we still have class?"

"We still have to study?"

"With *this* going on?!"

"Will you be grading our homework, too?"

"What about our food?"

Gern rattled his wings until the students were quiet.

"Jus' stick t' yer usual schedule! The school manages food all by itself, so that'll keep goin'. The stairs'll appear ev'ry afternoon, the doors'll unlock, all of it. But nothin' stops a Swickwit test, an' yeh've only got thir'een days to go. Whether everythin's back to normal 'round 'ere or not, you *will* be takin' it, an' the results *will* count."

The Nettle students shared gloomy looks as they absorbed this news.

"Now then," Gern continued. "Las' thing, an' most impor'ant: One of yeh'll need to be in charge."

Every eye fixed on the gargoyle.

Standing near the back of the crowd, Ava felt a rush of embarrassed excitement. She knew for certain whom Gern would choose. He knew her best out of everyone there, and he knew she could keep calm and complete a quest while wrangling her distractible friends. Carmelie and Dorian were bossy enough to lead, but they were clearly too mean, and the nicer kids like Matthew or Opal could never control the group. The *obvious* choice for leader had to be—

"Crow!"

The class gasped as one, then cheered, and all Ava's insides changed places as she suddenly found herself feeling indignant, guilty, let down, then finally happy for Crow, whose sweet, round face was turning very red.

"Wow, thanks!" he said. "That's so kind! Wait—does this mean I have to teach class?"

"No, no," said Gern. "Jus' be in charge an', you know, respons'ble. Yer the oldest one 'ere, after all. Only choice!"

The swirl in Ava's insides quieted. Gern had a point. It was wild how often she forgot that Crow was a whole two years older than the rest of them.

"But if no one is teaching," Margo asked, "how are we supposed to keep preparing for the Midwinter tests?"

"Tha's up to you to decide. With Crow leadin'."

Crow's face crinkled in a smile again.

"But," Gern went on, "there's one thing yeh abs'lutely mus' *not* do, an' that's try to tackle"—one giant finger stabbed upward at the maelstrom enveloping the school—"tha'. If the teachers an' Broom students couldn't 'andle it, there's no way you lot can, an' I won't lose any more students. Understood?"

His stony gaze raked over them all, stopping on Ava for a few extra, very meaningful seconds.

"Right, well." He shook out his shoulders. "Tha's one thing fixed. Ah'll be back same time termorrow t' see yer all still in one piece."

With the usual scraping of claws, Gern took off, swiftly disappearing among the towers of the school.

Beneath the raging storm the fourteen students of Nettle, together for the first time in seven weeks, and all on their own for the first time ever, looked at one another.

"Well," said Crow. "This should be interesting."

11

THE WAIT

Crow's first act as leader was to invite everyone back inside for a conference in the Round Room. The familiar space felt cozier than ever after the expanse of the roof, and it immediately became extra noisy.

To her surprise, Ava found herself sitting alone on one of the benches as Carmelie and Wolfgang grabbed Tinabella, filling her in on the storm and everything she'd missed; Henry and Jonsi put their heads together over a new epic poem; and the others all gathered around Crow, asking a hundred questions about how he was going to run things now that he was in charge.

Nobody was paying any attention to Ava at all.

She did not like it.

"I think we should vote on everything," Crow was saying, talking over the crowd. "Gern made me leader, not teacher or anything. I can just, you know, coordinate."

"What if there's a tie, though?" asked Dorian. "There are fourteen of us."

"Then Crow chooses," said Margo.

"But that's not fair!" Beryl snapped.

Crow waved his hands. "It's okay, we can figure out what works as we—"

"I don't think we should decide anything yet!" Carmelie interrupted from across the room. She had an arm over Tinabella's shoulders. "Not until Tinabella's cured and can tell us what she thinks."

Ava heard herself give a grumpy snort. "She can still nod, can't she?" she called. The old familiar left-out feeling was washing over her. Plus she didn't like the way Carmelie was already pushing at Crow. "Right, Tinabella?"

Tinabella shrugged.

"So what?" Carmelie retorted. "It's still not fair! How would you feel if you couldn't say exactly what you thought, Ava, and the rest of us started making all sorts of decisions without you?"

Ava felt her cheeks go hot as the faces of the class flipped back to her.

Carmelie was perfectly right.

"Whatever," she muttered. "Good point."

Crow looked like he was feeling the strain of leadership already.

"So . . . that's the plan? Does everybody agree we should wait to make any big decisions until Tinabella is better?"

There was a general round of agreement.

"Then I guess we're all, um, free until sundown," Crow said. "Right, Ava? You said Burdock's going to knock on the library door around then if he found a cure?"

Ava nodded.

"Great!" Crow clapped his hands. "Well, try not to get into trouble, everybody."

It was a very awkward morning.

As soon as the meeting ended, Tinabella shrugged off Carmelie's arm and beelined for her and Ava's room, still clutching the soup book. Ava hopped up to follow, then stopped short as the slam of their door echoed down the hall.

Well, maybe it would be a good idea to give Tinabella some space. After all, the last time Tinabella had been in their room she'd sneakily packed her bags, thinking she was about to leave school forever to become Vivienne Morderay's apprentice. It must have felt pretty weird returning seven weeks later clutching a giant cookbook and only able to speak in soupish.

No one wanted to try restarting their morning lessons—there was no way they could concentrate after everything that had happened—so they all just bounced around, filling in the time until the stairs reappeared and they could release some of their nervous energy running through the rest of the school.

Carmelie, Wolfgang, and Dorian camped out in the classroom beside the missing window, whispering together and laughing uproariously whenever anyone came in. Matthew and Opal practiced backward juggling in the Round Room with varying degrees of success. Margo and Beryl disappeared into their dorm rooms. Branwen announced she was going back to bed.

Jonsi and Henry invited Ava to work with them on their new poem, but she didn't last long. It was about the storm, and by the time she read through what they had so far, which started with *Oh, Swickwit, my Swickwit, storm-sunk and alone / Despair beats her wings in fate's spiral glow,* she realized she actually had some important doodling to do in her spell book.

Crow hovered over everyone, moving from group to group, checking how people were feeling, patting shoulders, and doing a serious amount of smiling until, to the entire tower's relief, lunch finally arrived.

It was a very long afternoon.

Tinabella made a brief appearance to grab food—a grilled cheese sandwich and whiffleberry pie—before disappearing back into their room. Ava followed after finishing her own meal, but her roommate barely glanced up from the ancient-looking leather tome she was reading on her bed.

"I'm, uh, gonna see if the boys want to visit the library," Ava said, with one hand on the door. "Or maybe try to spy on the Cobweb and Cauldron kids. Wanna join?"

Tinabella rolled her eyes.

"Okay," said Ava. "Do you want to sneak out and see what the storm looks like from beside the lake instead?"

Brittle paper crinkled as Tinabella turned the page.

"Cool." Ava was honestly confused. Tinabella had tried to *hug* her when she'd showed up in Punzell Tower. "Well, I'll let you settle in. It's, um, really good to have you back."

She was halfway out the door when she heard Tinabella murmur, "Add croutons. Serves two generously."

Ava glanced behind, but her friend's—frenemy's? what were they now?—expression was blank. Unless . . . was that a twitch at the corner of her mouth?

Daring a quick smile of her own, Ava nodded and left, closing the door behind her.

In the end she and the boys did go to the library. Crow wanted to track down any books on Swickwit operations that might help in his new role as leader, and Henry wanted to find more synonyms for *storm* he and Jonsi could use in their poem.

Ava had hoped the three of them might huddle up under their old table and talk over everything that was happening, but Crow was seriously distracted in his new role, and Henry was focused on his quest, and she didn't feel right asking them to stop just to keep her company.

Their table wasn't available, anyway, since the library turned out to be unusually crowded with older students. Cobweb and Cauldron kids appeared around every corner, scanning the shelves, yanking down books, or sending messages across the library with color-coded sparks. They completely ignored the Nettle students, of course, but that didn't stop their presence from making the visit much more difficult.

Once Ava stumbled directly into the middle of three Cobweb girls having what looked to be a furious argument, their faces contorted as they gestured at a pile of scrolls spread open between them. Their shield spell must have been perfect, because Ava couldn't hear a thing, and she jumped away quickly, her heart hammering.

Between that and a group of Cauldron boys competing to see who could balance the biggest stack of chairs on their chin, Ava, Crow, and Henry were ready to leave the library much earlier than usual.

Crow decided it was his duty to stay on-site at Nettle Tower after that, so Ava, still restless, talked Henry into joining her on a stress-relieving wander through the school.

They didn't talk much, but Ava had a nice time as they chucked pebbles into the slime fountain, conjured squirrel illusions for the ghost cats to chase, tried and failed to find the Bubbling Ballroom, and made the trek up to the Long Gallery to see the Moldy Horse.

"I wish the school was in Wicked Mode so we could talk to him," Ava said as the life-size paper horse they'd shared their big adventure with seven weeks ago continued his relentless, unseeing gallop up and down the stone corridor.

"I wish he lived with us in Nettle Tower," said Henry. "And

there was no storm and everyone was safe and we knew for a fact we were all going to pass our Midwinter testing."

"Oh wow." Ava let out a long sigh. "Me too."

It was a very tense dinner.

There were only the dozen Broom students missing from the student body, but the normal evening buzz was distinctly dampened. The dining hall felt larger than it should have, and if the Nettle students were sitting closer together than usual, nobody said anything about it.

The older students were acting much as they had in the library: talking and muttering in small groups, hurrying back and forth, gesturing and arguing with their heads together. Ava felt an uneasy tickle on the back of her neck as she watched them. They had to be plotting to take on the storm themselves, no matter what Gern had said. She watched them, wondering what weird, advanced magic they were planning.

What if they succeeded? Or worse, what if they didn't? What if they got caught like the rest? What if, in a week or so, she and the other Nettle students were all that was left of the entire school, sitting here alone at their table, the dark fortress echoing around them?

All in all, it was not the most relaxing dinner of Ava's life.

At least the food was good. It had been particularly good since the dining hall switched to its winter menu, and Ava had found all sorts of new favorites like green buckle pot pies, spicy honeycomb noodles, and grilled snow salad. Her plate that night was loaded up with fried fruitroot and sliced harph, with an extra-tasty bowl of caramel apple custard for dessert.

The only person disappointed in the menu was Crow, who was sad about the lack of soup and the lost chance to see if Tinabella could communicate with it.

"Well, can you blame me?" he said to Ava, when she elbowed him to stop going on about it. Tinabella was looking even more annoyed than usual. "This time tomorrow she'll hopefully be cured! What if she forgets how to speak soupish? We might be missing out on one of Oz's greatest secrets!"

At last the meal was over, the lights in the fortress windows dimmed, and it was nearly time to find out what hopefully Tinabella-fixing magic Burdock had in store for them.

12

THE CURE

Ava was relieved to be back in Nettle Tower after the somber mood in the dining hall. Margo and Beryl bustled off to change into pajamas, but most of her classmates milled around the Round Room, chatting nervously as they waited for Burdock.

Finally, the stairs vanished, a *schwuck* came from the library and laboratory doors as the portals closed, and a nervous anticipation filled the air.

Tinabella wore her usual half scowl, but Ava, sitting beside her on the floor, saw her knuckles whiten as she squeezed her arms around her knees.

"Will he be here right away?" Wolfgang asked.

Ava shook her head. "It could be a couple minutes. He only wakes up when it's night, so he might have to, you know, start his day or whatever."

Carmelie huffed. "It's so weird that you've all talked to this librarian and no one else has ever even seen him."

"Yeah," said Jadis. "What's he like?"

Ava was trying to figure out how to answer that when there was a loud knock, followed by another *schwuck*. Everyone scrambled to their feet.

"He's, uh, different," offered Henry as the library door swung open.

Most of the class screamed.

"Oh my!" yelped Burdock. His shiny black eyes blinked rapidly as he took in the crowd. "What a welcoming! And on this tragical night, too. Hello, Tinabella! I'm so relievered to see you back in the safety of your peers."

Tinabella waved, an actual smile on her face.

"And Ava, Crow, Henry," Burdock went on. "Yes, goodly. Now, will those who are still screameling kindly stop?"

The uproar trailed off.

"Thanking you." Burdock rustled his wings. "This has been the most upsetting wakening I can rememberify in centuries. I had barely openized my eyes before the school was filling me in about the storming and the poor teachers and students. Warden Pike will find a way to fixify everything, of course, but this is still truly upsettitizing."

The class stared at him. Tinabella nudged Ava forward, and she cleared her throat. "Um, Burdock? Did you happen to find—"

"Oh! Yes!" The librarian rummaged in his wing case and pulled out a large piece of parchment. "I believe I have found a curing for Tinabella. I spent all last night researchering exorcisms and banishingments, then finally remembered the simplest little librarian spell for the cleanation of parasites out of books."

"Parasites?" said Crow.

"Parasites?" said Ava.

"*Garlic croutons?*" said Tinabella, looking very offended.

"Yes!" Burdock beamed. "It shows enormous effectivity at getting living things that shouldn't be in books out again. You know, paper squids and minimillion mites—that sortness of thing."

Henry raised a hand. "But isn't it the other way round here? Isn't the cookbook kind of haunting Tinabella?"

Burdock waved three of his arms. "No, no. Pleasingly remember, *she* tried to smuggle herself *into* it. The results are surprisifying, I'll grant you, but she is the one in the book, and this spelling should resolve that."

"Okay, great!" said Crow. "What happens now? Are you doing the spell?"

Burdock smiled. "I could," he said, drawing out the word. "But I have an amusifying idea. The spell requires six hands to performulate. I have six hands." He waggled them. "So do you."

Ava, Crow, and Henry looked at one another, realizing as they did that the rest of the class had fallen back, leaving the three of them and Tinabella alone around Burdock.

"You want *us* to cure Tinabella?" Crow asked.

"Really?" Henry peeped.

"Why not? It's a simple incantanation. Nothing a Nettle student couldn't handle!"

"Teaspoon, teaspoon, teaspoon," cut in Tinabella, her arms clamped around the soup book. She thrust her chin at Ava and the boys. "Pulp nine butter grapes and fourteen watersplots!"

"Now, now." Burdock made a calming gesture. "I'm surety that your friends will do a fine job. It's only group magic, after all!"

Ava had been opening her mouth to say no to the librarian's reckless idea, but at the words *group magic,* a tingle ran up her spine. She thought of the wild-haired Broom girl leading her classmates in their attack on the storm. She'd looked so strong and powerful with everyone following. So respected.

"I guess, maybe?" she said, looking to Crow and Henry, who shifted uncertainly.

"Do it!" someone yelled from the benches. "Woo!" There was a smattering of applause.

"Um, Tinabella?" Ava asked.

She interpreted Tinabella's eye-roll-shrug-huff combo as grudging acceptance.

"Well, cool," Ava said, taking the lead along with the parchment from Burdock. "Let's see what we've got."

Burdock hadn't been lying; it really was a simple spell. All they had to do was cast a circle of protection around Tinabella and the soup book, then tap their fingers together—each pair of hands doing a different pattern—while chanting the words off the scroll.

The words meant nothing to Ava, but they were fun to say:

Griddle middle hiddle widdle
Scotty-otty ooo.
Liddle biddle viddle riddle
Otty-scotty scoo.

They chanted and tapped, awkwardly at first, then slowly finding their rhythm. Tinabella sat in the center of the circle, the book open in front of her and her face set.

As the spell took hold, Ava could feel her magic reaching out for Henry's and Crow's. There was a shimmery, wobbly sensation before they merged, then, to her utter surprise, she suddenly *saw* her two dear friends' magic through her inner eye. It was a bit like connecting with the boiling lake or the river by the Yellow Brick Road, only much more vivid and complex.

Crow's magic was optimistic, bright, and hopeful, yet strangely confined. Looking closer, she realized he was keeping back anything connected to Bone Fire. From what she could tell, that meant he was cutting himself off from most of his magical strength, all the time, on purpose. All to protect the people around him.

Henry's magic was fascinating. At first glance it was worryingly thin and shaky—he was clearly nervous about messing up the spell—but everywhere Ava looked there were deep pockets of color, like pools of untapped power. She was astonished at how different Henry's magic was from Crow's until she remembered: Henry wasn't just a witch, he was also a cursed giant prince.

She wondered if the boys were reading anything about her, and what they might find. Curious, she turned her magical attention on herself.

The scars on her hands began to tingle . . .

Then there was a flash of light, a *whumph* of vinegar-scented air, and Tinabella and the soup book were hurled apart.

"Successosity!" cheered Burdock, magicking the book into his arms. "Grandly done, you three. I knew you could do it!"

Ava, Crow, and Henry shook out their fingers while everyone turned to Tinabella, who was picking herself up and brushing off her robes.

"Well, Tinabella," Burdock called. "How do you feel? What words of wisdomiration have you been dying to expressify to all your young friends?"

The whole Round Room waited. Ava pushed down a smile. Tinabella always had plenty to say, and after seven weeks with only teachers to talk to, she must have been bursting with things to get off her chest.

Tinabella glanced around, nodding once at Burdock. "Great," she said. "Good night."

Without another word she turned and disappeared down the hall, slamming the door behind her.

13

TINABELLA'S APOLOGY

"What was that?!" demanded Ava, bursting into their room a minute later.

Tinabella, who'd been pacing the floor between their beds, spun to face her.

"You didn't even say thank you to Burdock!" Ava continued. "He says good night, by the way. He also warned us to not try and tackle the storm, and—"

"Ugh, will you just let me talk?!"

Ava stopped, her mouth hanging open.

"I've been stuck speaking soupish for two days," said Tinabella, her hands on her hips. "I haven't talked normally to another kid in seven weeks, and the second I'm back, my roommate starts lecturing my elbows off!"

Ava closed her mouth.

"Thanks," said Tinabella. "Anyway, I wanted to start by saying I know what you're thinking, and you can stop worrying, I'm not mad anymore. I decided to forgive you."

For a moment the world went so quiet Ava could hear the storm outside.

"Wait," she said. "*You* forgive *me*? For what?"

"For making Vivienne Morderay like you better.

For being the apprentice she actually wanted."

"How is that *my* fault?" Ava was so shocked she was seeing stars. "It's got nothing to do with me! I should be the one saying if I forgive *you*!"

Tinabella bristled. "Oh yeah? What for?"

Ava pressed her hands to her head. "Oh, maybe for trying to betray the whole school, for tricking me and Crow and Henry, for giving the wickedest witch in Oz the one thing she needed to get even more powerful, for—"

"Ugh! Fine, whatever! *Sorry!*"

The two girls crossed their arms, staring each other down across the room.

Sounds of their classmates heading to bed drifted in from outside, voices and doors closing along the hall.

All at once Ava realized her long weeks living solo were over; she wouldn't be alone in the dark that night. She was surprised how glad that made her.

Almost against her will, her frustration with Tinabella drained away.

"Cool," she said. "Well, welcome back, I guess. How, uh, how was it?"

Tinabella gave Ava one of her looks before flopping onto her bed.

"You saw Punzell Tower. How do you think it was?"

"Not great?"

"Mm-hmm. You have no idea how slow time can go

when you're stuck in one place. Luckily, I kept myself busy."

Ava huffed a laugh. "What, plotting your revenge?"

"Exactly."

Ava's smile slipped.

"I'm serious," Tinabella said. "Remember what I told you I always get?"

"You always get revenge on people who mess with you."

"That's right. So I kept busy studying, researching every possible way of taking Vivienne Morderay down. Or at least messing with her hold on that Collar of Arboc thing."

Ava felt her eyebrows leap up. As far as she knew, Vivienne was now the most powerful witch in all of Oz. Warden Pike might be a match for her in a fair fight, but then again maybe not. Ava herself had been wildly powerful for a few minutes down in the Bitter Forge—she could still remember the joy of it; it had felt so *right*—but even then, would she have been a match for the glamorous wicked witch who'd locked their school in this unstoppable storm?

"I read so many books in that tower, Ava. Old ones. The kind that smell like anteater elbows and make your eyelids itch. Burdock brought me whatever I wanted, and I read it all."

Ava noticed the tone of Tinabella's voice had changed. So had her gaze. There was a razor focus to her now. It was a little intimidating.

"And, uh, did you find anything?" Ava asked. "Any magic that could take on Viv?"

Tinabella's smile was so perfectly poised between wicked and good, it made Ava shiver.

"Just one, but luckily there are lots of ways of using it." Tinabella pulled a scroll from her robes, unfurling it so it rolled across her bed and onto the floor. Block letters across the top read *VIVIENNE REVENGE PLAN*. "So I made a list."

14

TINABELLA'S PLAN

"Whoa!" Ava eyed the dense scribbles filling Tinabella's revenge scroll. "You seriously found this many ways to tackle Vivienne?"

"Kind of. Here, stop hovering all weird like that and sit down."

Tinabella scooched over, and Ava settled beside her on the bed, feeling awkward but pleased.

"My plan's based on this thing I read about called *arcane resonance*," Tinabella went on. "Turns out any time a witch is magically controlling something far away, there's this link that opens between them. Like a thread that keeps the connection working."

Ava thought. "Is that like with my mirror? How Vivienne could eavesdrop while her magic was powering it, but not after?"

"Exactly. She could listen in because of the link. But"—Tinabella gave a wolfish grin—"it turns out the connection is vulnerable. People who know what they're doing can use the thread to mess with the witch powering the other end. As soon as I read that, I was like, *Yes! That is how I'm getting revenge on Vivienne.* You don't even know how excited I was when I got out and saw this storm. I thought I was gonna have to wait until Vivienne showed up again, but her magic is literally parked right outside."

"You're sure there's a link back to her in the storm, then?" Ava asked.

"Has to be! And I'd bet anything she used that collar to cast it." She rattled the scroll. "I'm certain I can get at least one of these to jumble both of them up good."

Ava eyed her roommate. "You really have been thinking about this the whole time, haven't you?"

Tinabella sat up. "Seven weeks, Ava! Vivienne abandoned me after I did *everything* for her. Then *bam,* seven weeks in that tower. Just me, my books, and lectures from Pike and Mulch." She slumped back against the wall. "I'm almost as happy they're gone as I am for the storm. No classes or homework or anything while I make Vivienne pay? Thank you, Oz."

It was Ava's turn to sit up. "Hang on, didn't anybody tell you?" she said. "We're still having class and everything in the morning. And we've been doing study groups instead of clubs in the afternoon. There's only twelve full days left until Midwinter testing, and we all have to pass. For real."

"Seriously?" Tinabella looked like she'd swallowed a mouthful of sour leeches. "I thought Carmelie was joking about that. Well, fine, we'll see how it goes, but I'm not letting some random test get in the way of my plans. Not when things are this perfect."

She turned to the window, staring out into the night. "This is my chance to finally make everything the way it should be, Ava. Chances like this only come by once in a lifetime." Her bangs swung as her head snapped back. "So, are you with me?"

Ava gaped at her.

"Come on," Tinabella urged. "Let the rest of them keep doing their study prep or whatever. We've got a mission to complete." She broke into a sudden smile. "It'll be like old times!"

A warm spark flared inside Ava, growing quickly to an excited glow.

A secret magical mission sounded like just what she needed. She hadn't exactly been happy with all the extra schoolwork lately, and besides, her test preparations were going fairly okay. Twelve days was kind of a lot if you thought about it. Didn't she deserve a little distraction?

As for taking on the storm, sure, Gern had told them not to, but he hadn't known about Tinabella's research when he said that. He hadn't known there might be a real, genuine way to beat Vivienne. And wasn't that the most important thing right now?

"I don't know," she said, playing for time. "What about Henry and Crow? Could they help? We could all do it together."

"While Professor Crow is in charge of the class?" Tinabella shook her head. "Absolutely not."

Ava sighed. "I guess he probably would try to talk us out of it. And Henry would tell Crow anything we told him."

"Exactly."

"Can I look over the list first, at least?" Ava asked. "Just to see if it's stuff I think I could do?"

Tinabella flapped a hand. "I'll walk you through the details tomorr-o-ow," she said, ending on a yawn. "It's basically just different variations on curses, poisons, and entanglement—you know, taking over someone's mind and body."

"Aren't those all kind of, well, wicked?"

"Um, yeah! We have to outdo *Vivienne Morderay*. What, too tough for you?"

"I just—I don't think I've ever done, like, deliberately wicked magic before," said Ava.

"Oh no, of course, all the wicked things *you've* done have been by accident!" Tinabella could have earned a medal for eye rolling. "Look, if you don't want to help, fine. But I'm going to try. It's going to be hard, though. There'll be tons of dangerous spell ingredients to find and blend, and super cool dark magic rituals to do, and special tools to make. And Warden Pike could come back any minute, so I probably won't succeed if I have to do it all on my own. I could totally miss my chance." She tilted her face dramatically to the ceiling. "If only I had a friend by my side . . ."

"You are so ridiculous," said Ava, grinning despite herself. She bit her lip, pretending to think, but really she'd already decided.

She nodded.

"Good!" Tinabella said. "Now get off my bed so I can get some sleep, you monster. Things are gonna get wicked busy around here starting tomorrow."

Lying snug in her own bed a few minutes later, listening to the muffled roar of the storm as she stared into the dark, Ava tried to sort out what had happened that evening. A day of nonstop surprises had ended with what might be the best one of all: Tinabella, back in her life as a friend. Okay, a friend tugging her along on a risky, complicated, possibly impossible mission that would definitely involve breaking a heap of school rules. But wasn't that classic Tinabella?

If this worked, if the two of them really conquered Vivienne Morderay's storm, maybe even the wicked witch herself, Ava knew they would go down in history as the most remarkable students Swickwit had ever seen.

Not bad for a little extra hard work and danger, she thought as sleep tugged her under. Not bad at all.

15
VIVIENNE

Floating in her crystal-and-platinum bathtub in a cloud of rose steam and opal bubbles, amethyst candles twinkling all around and the last Calabrian harp in Oz singing her a song kings and queens had once handed over their crowns to hear, Vivienne Morderay yawned.

Calling down Dorothy's Gale on Swickwit had taken a surprising amount of magical energy, and she was resting to rebuild her strength before sweeping across Oz in a reign of wicked glory.

Which she would, of course, once she was done with this bath. And once she sorted out exactly what she'd like to do. There were endless options: steal every wedding ring in Winkie Country to pave her front walk, turn the Emerald City a dull maroon, transform all the giants into rock candy. Only none of these ideas seemed quite right. Quite *enough*.

Casting Dorothy's Gale had been immensely satisfying, at least. The Lost Collar of Arboc had glowed a dazzling, celestial white around Vivienne's neck, and she'd laughed and laughed, picturing the shock and dismay on the faces of everyone trapped in her old school.

That little counterspell from the teachers had been especially amusing. For one surprising moment it had almost worked, but, of course, nothing could stop the gale or the collar, and into the storm the teachers went, doomed to sleep spinning round and round until the end of Vivienne or the end of Oz, whichever came first.

The capture of the twelve Broom students shortly after had left her sighing in delight. If only Warden Pike had been caught, too, her revenge would have been complete. She gave him credit for being cautious enough not to touch the storm, but it did seem odd that he'd allowed his staff and students to put themselves in danger. He must be losing his touch.

Well, it was about time. Threnody Pike had been ancient when Vivienne was at school, and that was a hundred years ago.

Unbidden and unwelcome, images of her arrival at Swickwit drifted like the perfumed steam through her mind.

Vivienne flinched at the memory of herself then: a small, sickly purple girl with mousy-blah hair and white, unremarkable teeth.

The other children had seemed so confident as they jostled her in the Wicked Wagon, though that had changed when they reached the school. Her classmates gaped at their grim surroundings, but Vivienne narrowed her eyes. She was the child of carnival workers—before her magic, she'd been destined for a life selling caramel corn and peanuts—and she knew a performance when she saw one. When Warden Pike made his big show of lifting Wicked Mode, revealing the true nature of the school, Vivienne had taken her first lesson at Swickwit thoroughly to heart: Grown-ups are not to be trusted.

Her classmates had been the usual mix—some who thought they were good, some who knew they were wicked—but all of them had laughed at her when she demonstrated her first magic. True, tangling up people's shoelaces wasn't that impressive, but at the time it was all she had. She'd absorbed her second lesson then, standing alone at the front of the Nettle classroom: Strength is the only thing that matters.

Her classmates weren't laughing long. Vivienne made it her business to become the most remarkable student Swickwit had ever seen, and within a month each of them had learned that she was not to be mocked, not to be trusted, and not to be messed with.

That had been the start of it, the first steps of her climb to become the most powerful, most celebrated, wickedest witch in all of Oz. Wickeder than Osmuth Rust. Wickeder than Filbert the Cruel. Wickeder than that overhyped West Oz witch whose name was thankfully muddled by history: Gregoria Maggery, or Magrat Hamlytown, maybe. No one was sure.

Whatever their names, Vivienne was the worst of the

worst now. She had enhanced her own magic with Oz's rarest and most wonderful artifacts, wielding extraordinary powers as effortlessly as she floated in this priceless bathtub. All her work had paid off. All her dreams had come true. Her life was perfect.

She yawned again, then sighed, scratching a frowny face into the side of the tub with one razor-sharp nail.

So why did *perfect* leave her feeling like . . . this?

A sound came from the window, and Vivienne snapped her beautiful head up to see a bedraggled mustard bird scrabbling at the sill. She huffed, disappointed. Why couldn't it have been something interesting like a venomous kite or an enemy attack?

She peered closer at the visitor, and her eyebrows met. Was that the same bird she'd seen the day before?

One wave of her hand and the visitor was inside her lair, locked in an elaborate gold cage.

The bird hissed at her, then coughed, hacking up a few feathers.

"Well!" called Vivienne. "That's no way for a guest tooo behave."

Another wave, and the bird slumped down, unconscious and, because Vivienne was in a generous mood, no longer dull yellow but bright purple with fuchsia zigzags.

Vivienne leaned back amid the rose-scented opal bubbles, magicking the water a little hotter, the harp a little louder, and the candles just a little sparklier. The bird could wait for now. Oz could wait for now. Being perfectly wicked was hard work, and there was no sense rushing her plans.

She would get to it all once her full strength was back.

Just as soon as she finished this bath.

16

CROW'S PEP TALK

Breakfast in Nettle Tower the next morning was noisy.

A giddy, nervous energy filled the air, and there was plenty of laughter and running up and down the hall as the students geared up for their first full day without grown-up supervision.

Ava and Tinabella caused a bit of a scene when they wandered in, grabbed food, and sat side by side on one of the benches. Carmelie and Dorian, who'd clearly been saving a spot for Tinabella, slid together, whispering, and Jadis openly stared with a look of mingled suspicion and surprise.

Ava couldn't help feeling a little thrill at the attention. There was something about Tinabella choosing her out of everyone that made her feel special. Important.

Crow was nowhere to be seen, but Henry and Jonsi came over to sit with Ava and Tinabella, their plates loaded with fried ostridon eggs and tinselberry pancakes.

"Hi," Henry said. "How's it going, Tinabella? Um, being back?"

Ava blinked at Henry's boldness—then remembered he and Tinabella had shared the quest to reset Nettle Tower. Tinabella had even complimented his courage in the spiny scab flea room.

"It's whatever," Tinabella answered. "It's not like any of this is new. Well"—she waved her fork at the countdown clock, now glowing with a luminous 12—"except that, obviously."

Ava shook her head. "It's so annoying we're still supposed to take the test."

"Trust Swickwit to have a backup system," snorted Tinabella.

"You don't think we'll really be alone for twelve more days, do you?" Henry said. "Warden Pike will fix things before then, right?"

Ava felt another thrill as she and Tinabella shared a look. If everything went to plan, it wouldn't be Warden Pike doing the fixing.

"It shouldn't take that long," said Tinabella.

"Maybe not long at all," Ava said.

"I think being on our own will be good for us," Jonsi said unexpectedly, his eyes fixed on the ceiling. "We can finally try our strength against the upside-down dust ducks."

Ava followed his gaze but saw nothing. She was just opening her mouth to ask what an upside-down dust duck was when the classroom door cracked open.

Crow's head appeared, and the hubbub in the Round Room quieted.

"Hi, everyone!" he said. "Okay, so, uh, please enter! Class is now in session!"

* * *

Most of the Nettle students took their usual desks in the classroom, including Ava and Tinabella. Carmelie, Dorian, Wolfgang, and Jadis pushed theirs together against the back wall, sitting on top of them with their arms crossed.

Crow stood in Professor Mulch's spot up front. There were dark shadows under his eyes and a nervous grin on his face, and the chalkboard beside him was covered in writing. The roaring storm outside thundered in through the missing window, but they were all getting used to the sound by now.

"Right, morning!" Crow said. "Did everybody sleep well?"

The class exchanged glances. A few people shrugged.

"I didn't," offered Crow. "I was up all night getting ready!"

"It shows!" called Carmelie from the back of the room.

Some kids laughed. Others shushed her.

"Okay, well," Crow went on. "I know it's weird that Gern put me in charge. Yeah, I am the oldest, but I'm also the worst student here. No"—he held up a hand as Ava and Margo protested—"it's true. And you're probably all really worried about passing your tests now because of that. I mean, what could I teach any of you? Apart from juggling, I mean." He paused, his eyes shining. "But I think I figured out how we can totally do this."

Ava waited, and realized that the rest of the room was waiting quietly, too. Somehow, Crow had earned the class's respect without any of Professor Mulch's usual shouting.

"It all comes from what Professor Mulch was telling us right before the storm hit," Crow continued. "I was super inspired by what she said about focusing on our weakest parts and leveling up fast. So"—he flourished both hands at the chalkboard—"I made this! It's a chart showing all the most important things we'll be tested on."

Ava examined the board and saw a row of subjects written across the top—*Protection Spells, Magical Plants & Fungi, History of Prophecy,* and more, with a dozen or so lines drawn under each. The first line under every subject said *Crow.*

"What are the blank lines for?" Branwen asked.

"That's where our names go," Crow said. "We'll all sign up under the things we want to get better at, then erase our names once we've done it."

"You want us to admit what we're worst at?" said Beryl. "Right in front of everybody?"

Crow shook his head. "Try to think about it like Professor Mulch said: Where can we make the most progress the fastest? Look, I went first. I put my name under *everything.*"

There was a murmur of interest, and Ava smiled to herself. Crow's cheerful honesty was putting everyone at ease.

"Who's gonna teach us how to get better?" Wolfgang called from the back of the room. "Since it's obviously not you."

"Manners!" Tinabella snapped.

"Great question," said Crow. "I thought we could ask for volunteers; whoever feels confident on a subject can teach the rest of us. We could always vote, too, but I think volunteers would be best."

"So we're teaching each other now?" said Opal.

"Only if you want to," answered Crow.

More murmurs filled the room.

"I guess I could take light magic," Carmelie said, raising her hand.

"Ooh, yes!" Dorian nodded. "I'm super jealous of your dark rainbows."

"Wolfgang should be in charge of magical plants and fungi," Carmelie went on. "He's got all of them memorized. And Jadis has temperature charms down cold . . ."

Carmelie's interest helped kick things off, and soon all the subjects were spoken for.

"Awesome, excellent!" said Crow. His eyes were shining again. "So, are we doing this? Everybody ready to help each other level up?"

His answer was a scraping of chairs as everyone rose to crowd around the board.

Margo got the chalk last, and she was just putting a final flourish on her name under Matthew's mathcantations class when there was a heavy thump and rattle from overhead.

The Nettles all scrambled up the roots to the roof—even Henry did okay this time—where they found a harassed-looking Gern waiting for them.

He shared what news there was: no change in the storm, the Cauldron and Cobweb students were a serious handful, and an infestation of hiccuping prune moths had been discovered in the entrance hall.

When he was done, Crow proudly filled Gern in on their new self-directed study plan.

"And it was all Crow's idea!" said Ava.

"He's really good at being in charge," Matthew said.

"I'm teaching temperature charms," noted Jadis.

"Fine, fine," said the gargoyle, waving one huge stone hand. He seemed very distracted. Ava thought she could make out new wrinkles around his eyes. "Jus' stay safe an' keep out o' trouble. An' don' go messin' with that storm!"

Back in the classroom there was some confusion about how to start their new level-up program, and Crow took the lead again by tackling the schedule.

This turned out to be seriously complicated, since not everyone signed up for everything, and the volunteer teachers needed a chance to learn from one another, too. But somehow Crow worked it all out, and soon the class had a neat, organized chart on the blackboard covering the full morning hours and the first hour after lunch.

The only real problem was a shortage of room, but that was solved when Jadis reluctantly agreed to allow the rest of them into the lab once the portal doors unlocked in the afternoon. Ava and Tinabella shared a grin. Neither of them had ever seen inside the lab, nor had anyone else since Jadis claimed it for herself at the start of the year and placed a curse on it that wrapped intruders in cocoons of frozen asparagus.

Crow came over to Ava and Tinabella as the class split in two, some to review astral basics with Opal at their desks, the rest to brush up on circles of protection with Branwen in the Round Room.

"How am I doing?" he asked under his breath.

"Great!" whispered Ava.

"Eh, not bad," said Tinabella.

Henry joined them. "You're super good at this, Crow!"

"Thanks!" Crow looked nervous and proud. "It's tough. But I think it might be going okay."

"You're a natural," Ava said firmly.

Crow beamed, then, "Oh, hey," he called, yelling over the chatter. "Don't forget we've only got twenty minutes for each subject before we switch around again!"

"So make 'em count!" yelled Branwen from the Round Room, making everybody laugh.

"And you," Tinabella said, leaning in to whisper in Ava's ear, "don't forget we've got our own project to tackle the second these study groups are over."

Ava nodded, her head spinning at how busy she suddenly was.

Pass the test, keep the secret, prove a point, and save the school?

Tinabella had been right: It *was* like old times.

17

THE LABORATORY

The rest of the morning flew by, and Ava found herself having an unexpectedly wonderful time. The whole class had come together over Crow's plan, and with only twenty minutes to spend on each mini lesson, there wasn't room for nerves or distraction or anything besides instant learning. Most fascinating of all, each student teacher turned out to have a completely different way of explaining their magic.

"So you just push the resonance as far as it will go," Branwen said, in the Round Room session on circles of protection. "And you sort of tie the energy off, then make sure you hold the image in your mind. It's easier if you picture it glowing, or buzzing, kind of. Everybody want to try? Yes! That's better, Ava!"

Out of everyone, though, Dorian's teaching method was truly unique.

"You know how two plus two equals four?" he said, demonstrating a drying spell on a sopping-wet towel. "Well, this spell works like if two plus two equaled three thirty-five on a Wednesday afternoon."

Ava had been relieved at the other blank stares happening all around her.

Matthew raised a hand. "Is that like if we called socks *hats*, and hats *erasers*?"

"I don't know." Dorian shrugged. "Give it a try."

"It makes my brain feel like your example," said Matthew. "So maybe . . ." He waved his hand, and the towel was suddenly dry.

"Looks like that works!" said Dorian.

In the end they'd all come up with their own version of *two plus two equals 3:35 on a Wednesday afternoon*. Ava's had been *the color of wet sand under moonlight*, and while her drying spells weren't really good enough yet, it was more progress than she'd made in weeks.

By the time lunch rolled around, the whole class was giddy with early success, and they all dived hungrily on their apple-salad sandwiches and caramel cloudcake. Ava found herself seated next to Dorian, realizing as she ate that this was the most she'd ever talked and mingled with some of her classmates. The Nettles had never arranged themselves in such random combinations before, with Jonsi teaching Wolfgang how to improve his candle spells and Carmelie and Margo laughing together when their attempt at a homemade seat-warmer spell turned the nearest chair into a pile of ash.

As it turned out, it was all rather nice.

After lunch the portal doors unlocked, and everyone clapped as Jadis, grumbling, removed the curse from the laboratory entrance.

"Just don't judge me, okay?" she said, turning to glare at the watching class. "I didn't know I'd be having, like, guests today."

Ava, Henry, and Tinabella were all in the first lesson in the lab, and they pushed eagerly inside with the rest.

The lab turned out to be a rectangular room with whitewashed walls, a stone floor, and a row of half-moon windows looking out at a tangle of sticker vines and ivy in a courtyard Ava had never seen before. The air smelled sharp and sweet, with a mineral dustiness behind it. There were sinks and burners and long stone counters and shelves and shelves of bottles, which got Ava an elbow in the ribs and an excited whisper of "Poison supplies!" from Tinabella.

There was also, surprisingly, an elaborate and very cozy-looking pillow fort taking up one entire corner of the space.

Ava worked hard not to smile. Jadis was one of the scariest kids in their year—her first magic had been freezing stone so cold it shattered—and it was wild realizing she'd been hiding something like this.

"The pillow fort's new," Jadis said as they settled down, apparently unable to turn off her embarrassment. "It's just for, you know, winter."

Their temperature charms class didn't go quite as smoothly as their earlier ones. Ava suspected everyone might have been running out of steam, plus the lab itself was incredibly distracting. It was hard to listen to Jadis when there were so many jars and bottles to stare at, some glowing, some crowded with lumpy floating things, some rattling around on their own. The sinks, bowls, and burners were just as bad. Every time Ava looked up, they were in different places, though she never spotted one moving no matter how hard she tried. The whole lab seemed to be alive and fidgety, and the mood was definitely contagious.

Ava, Tinabella, and the boys were split up for their next two mini-classes, and then it was finally free time as their lessons for the day were over.

Many of their classmates chose to keep practicing what they'd learned, running with the momentum Crow had created, but Tinabella grabbed Ava by the elbow and marched her back to their room.

"Bye, Henry!" Ava called over her shoulder. "We'll see you later!"

Henry looked up from his conversation with Jonsi and gave a brief smile and thumbs-up. Crow was heading back into the classroom with Margo and Dorian, the three of them already juggling a complicated new cascade pattern. No one else was watching.

Ava felt a tiny bit miffed. If she was going to hide away from the group with Tinabella so they could work on their incredibly secret plans to out-wicked Vivienne Morderay and defeat the storm in the process, her classmates could at least be nosy about it.

18

POISON PREPARATIONS

Back in their room Tinabella unrolled her scroll across Ava's bed.

"Okay," she said. "So I think we should work out a schedule like the one Crow made. He can be annoyingly cheerful sometimes, but that was a really good idea."

"I still don't exactly know what we're doing," said Ava. "Last night you said you researched a bunch of curses and poisons and . . . what was the last one?"

"Entanglement. It's all in here." She patted the scroll.

"And we're going to use arcade remnants—"

"Arcane resonance."

"Right, that. We'll use that to send all the wicked stuff we're doing back at Vivienne? And hopefully it will overload the storm and, if we're lucky, maybe damage the collar?"

"Basically, yeah." Tinabella bounced on her toes, a gleam in her eye. "After seven weeks of planning by myself in that room, it's finally time for the big stuff." She stopped bouncing, her expression turning serious. "But we have to give it everything we've got. I am not missing this chance to get my revenge on Vivienne, and Warden Pike is not allowed to beat us to it."

"You got it," Ava said. Her brain felt jam-packed after the long morning, but she was definitely ready to be known as the girl who helped save the school. "Where do we start?"

Tinabella grinned and pointed to the top of the scroll. "With poison."

Ava's eyebrows met. "Why there? We don't even have any."

"Because it's the easiest one to deal with. In *Deadly Drinks to Know and Avoid,* Rodgort Stronge says true poison is basically like liquid magic. It has its own energy, which means we won't have to use any of ours. All we have to do is find it or make it, then chuck it into the storm."

"Oh." Ava had a sudden mental picture of the two of them hurling dark, sticky bottles at the wind. "That sounds doable, I guess. How many poisons do you think we'll need?"

Tinabella patted the scroll again. "All of them."

There were ten vicious poisons on Tinabella's scroll. They divided them up, with Tinabella responsible for finding or brewing Blue Zobbleth, Hitch-hetch, Bitter Wish, Drywax, and Wrathspool, and Ava taking charge of Sweet Ivy, Juthilamine, Timmy's Complaint, Krlthlgore, and Briner's Sponge.

The laboratory seemed like the obvious place to start, so the two of them skipped dinner that night and raided the shelves of glowing, hissing bottles. It was a harrowing business. One bottle stuck to Ava's fingers as soon as she touched it, and Tinabella had to use a ward charm to get it off. Another made Tinabella's hair scream until she put it down, and one squat little octagonal vial scampered up Ava's arm and tried to pour itself down her ear. Luckily, she got her hand in the way in time and Tinabella sent the bottle flying with a thwack of her spell book.

Most of the bottles were labeled, but there were a hundred kinds of handwriting to decipher, as well as more than a few languages. In the end, though, they were delighted to find five whole poisons from their list, making them halfway done already.

As they smuggled their haul back to their room, Ava wondered who had made all the poisons and why the teachers allowed them to remain in the lab. It seemed incredibly risky, even for a place where mummified hyenas could chase you down corridors and women made of needles could hold you captive beneath the school.

"Where were you?" wailed Crow when the rest of the class returned to find Ava and Tinabella lounging over a card game in the Round Room. "We had blue onion soup for dinner, Tinabella! It was the perfect chance to find out what it wants to tell us!"

"We weren't hungry," said Tinabella. Ava coughed as her stomach gave a loud growl at exactly the wrong moment. "And for the last time, Crow, I can't *talk to soup*. Soup doesn't have, like, advice, or opinions, or whatever. I was just stuck speaking in recipes for a while."

"But you haven't even tried yet!" said Crow. "This is Swickwit; anything could happen."

Later, as she and Tinabella were getting ready for bed, Ava crossed the poisons they'd found off their list. "So what about the five that are left?" she asked. "We still need Timmy's Complaint, Hitch-hetch, Juthilamine, Drywax, and Bitter Wish."

"We'll have to brew them ourselves," called Tinabella from their tiny bathroom. "The recipes are in the scroll."

Ava scanned Tinabella's craggy handwriting until she found the steps and ingredients for each one. She whistled.

"These are seriously complicated," she called. "Do you think we should just stick with the poisons we have?"

Tinabella emerged, shaking her head. "No way. We have to give it our all. If we go hard now and it works, we won't have to mess with curses or entanglement at all."

"Well, okay, I guess. But we'll definitely need someplace out of the way to put it all together."

Tinabella nodded. "It's a good thing we've spent plenty of time exploring the school then, isn't it?"

In the end, it took two more days to brew the final five poisons.

"Do you realize how lucky we got?" said Ava, stirring another handful of powdered cabbage bones into her cauldron as she worked on Timmy's Complaint. "I was looking at

Wrathspool and Briner's Sponge, and they take months to brew. For Krlthlgore you have to say the entire Mystoria Tumnaria spell without stopping or messing up once, and I don't think we would have had time to memorize all that."

"For sure." Tinabella's hair was going frizzy from the fumes coming off her own cauldron, but the instructions said it had to be stared at without blinking for ten seconds of every minute until it was finished, and Tinabella was not going to slip up now. "Super lucky."

They had set up their secret poison operation in the biggest of the ghost cat greenhouses. They'd never seen anyone else in there, and it was a reasonably open place with plenty of room for all their supplies.

Their cauldrons had been scavenged from the storeroom that once held the secret entrance to Warden Pike's portal clock room. The water came from the boiling lake, thanks to Ava, and the fire from a charm Tinabella had learned in detention. They hunted down the ingredients together.

Some poison components were easy to gather. Flaked mouse cane, pickled pecks, and saurian ooze powder were all available in the lab in tidy jars and baskets. Others, like lutch mold, which had to be scraped off walls with a piece of splintered bone, and wedge worm larva, which could only be coaxed out of drains with bare hands, made Ava's skin crawl.

It was all for a good cause, of course—defeating Vivienne would help everyone in Oz—but her stomach still twisted as she crushed wriggling blanch beetles into paste or weighed out stinking pine pus before stirring it into the brew.

Making poisons, it turned out, was actually a lot like making soup, and Tinabella's cookbook knowledge came in very handy for the technical aspects. Thanks to her, Ava learned the difference between a *simmer* and a *rolling boil*, as well as *beating* or *folding in* ingredients, and she tried her hardest to focus on those everyday details of their work: double-checking the recipe, monitoring heat levels, carefully following the steps.

Still, she couldn't ignore that there was something different about this magic. The ghost cats wouldn't come anywhere near their greenhouse, for a start. On the second day, a thin, faint screeching filled the air when they arrived, and the light seemed to be slowly dimming. The room itself began to feel denser, somehow, making Ava feel increasingly peculiar whenever she was inside it.

Once she looked over at Tinabella stirring her cauldron and gave a genuine yelp of fear. Her friend's hair was floating up around her face, her eyes huge, her smile wide, the light shining up from the fire drawing flickering patterns over her features. It was an alarming sight, and Ava wondered what *she* must look like after two days hunched over her own cauldron.

If she had to guess, she was probably starting to look pretty wicked, too.

* * *

Finally, on the evening of their second day of brewing, the missing poisons were done.

Timmy's Complaint was the bright fuchsia of plorange cotton candy, though when left to rest it quickly formed a crust of copper sparkles. Hitch-hetch was seven shades of brown at the same time. Juthilamine looked like plain water from straight on but glowed electric purple when glimpsed from the corner of your eye. Sky-blue Drywax had a thin column of red running through its center. Bitter Wish, oddly, was green-and-orange plaid.

Tinabella's friend Rodgort Stronge had certainly been right about true poison having its own energy. Ava could sense the powerful magic pulsing in every one of them, almost like their creations were alive. Alive and . . . eager.

"Excellent!" cackled Tinabella as Ava used her water powers to coax the poison into bottles. "Vivienne won't know what hit her!"

Elated with their success, the two friends put out the fires, shoved their cauldrons into a corner, and hurried back to Nettle Tower.

"What's that?" Beryl demanded, pointing at the bottle Ava was trying to hide behind her back as they slipped through the Round Room.

Ava's mind went blank.

"It's juicy-pop soda," Tinabella said, without missing a beat.

"I stole it off some Cauldron kids with my invisible running."

"Oh, I love juicy-pop soda!" called Opal. "Can I have some?"

"And me?" Dorian said.

"No way!" Tinabella declared, dodging past Wolfgang and Carmelie with Ava on her heels. "Night!"

Ava tossed a brief nod to Crow and Henry as she and Tinabella reached the hall. The boys were playing cards with Jonsi and Matthew, and both of them looked confused and even a little hurt at her hurried greeting.

She felt a pang of guilt but decided to ignore it. Sure, she'd been hanging out with them the whole time Tinabella was gone, and now she'd stopped with no explanation. But they couldn't expect her to keep them company every day, could they? Obviously things were going to be different now that her roommate was back.

This would all be worth it once she and Tinabella defeated Vivienne and the storm. Everything would be the way it was supposed to be: she would be famous, her friends would admire her, her place as an important witch would be secure.

And it could happen as soon as tonight.

19

THE POISONED STORM

A few hours later, when all their classmates were asleep and they couldn't stand to wait anymore, Tinabella and Ava tiptoed out of their room and down the hall, carrying their poison collection between them in a laundry basket.

Bottles clinked as they slid their way across the Round Room, and Ava winced, wishing she'd shoved more socks between them. But they reached the classroom without getting caught.

The constant howl of the storm grew louder as they opened the door and slipped through, closing it with a click behind them.

"Phew!" Ava whispered. "That was intense!" She really didn't want to have to explain what they were doing to any of their classmates. This was her and Tinabella's perfect chance to level up their status and make up for past mistakes. She definitely wasn't looking to share it.

Navigating the basket up to the roof was trickier than the two of them had expected. Ten full bottles made for heavy lifting, and for some reason the roots absolutely refused to touch the basket, so the two of them had to heave it up as they climbed. Finally, they reached the top and, lungs quaking, set the basket down at the base of the spike.

The storm seemed closer in the dark. There was no chance of seeing the stars, but a faint smear of light toward the south showed them where the moon must be, shining over the outside world.

For a moment Ava thought of the moonlight on the desert sand, and of her family. They would never understand what she was doing. Her whole world was far outside their understanding now.

Tinabella knelt down beside her, lining the bottles up and carefully removing the cork from each one. Pungent, skin-searing smells mingled in the still air.

"Hey, this isn't going to hurt the teachers and everyone spinning around in the storm, will it?" Ava asked.

Tinabella looked up. She'd conjured one of her lights, and her silver face looked wraithlike in the glow.

"Ava, seriously, they're trapped in a tornado of literal broken glass! Adding a bunch of poison can't possibly make things worse. Promise."

Ava swallowed. Their plan seemed much more reckless now that they were actually out here doing it. But she nodded.

The storm was too far out for them to throw the poison, so Ava had offered to float the bottles in using water from the lake. Now, though, she remembered the last time she'd flexed her powers from this roof.

She told Tinabella what had happened. "And I don't want

to get dizzy again," she finished. "Especially at night, and with the roots being all weird."

"Okay." Tinabella dropped the last cork into the empty laundry basket. "But couldn't you just toss the bottles in and let go of the water right away?"

Ava bit her lip. The fumes off the poison were making her feel odd, and she was genuinely nervous about getting her magic near the storm. But they'd made all this effort, and if she didn't try, they had no other way to deliver the poison. This part of the plan depended totally on her. Anxious or not, she really didn't have a choice.

It was still strange to see the lake without its fog, usually visible even at night. Ava gazed down at the bubbling water, settling into her magic as she ordered herself to just take things one step at a time.

The lake was behaving normally, at least, and she slowly pulled a coiling rope of water up, up, up over the school to where they were standing.

Tinabella grunted. "I haven't seen you do that before. With the lake, I mean. It's actually weird you're that powerful with water."

"Um, thanks?" said Ava, concentrating.

"I might have to do some research on it."

"Mm."

Ava was too busy to listen to Tinabella. The rope of water had risen from the lake easily enough, but now it was . . . resisting.

It seemed the water didn't want to get anywhere near their collection of poison. Ava couldn't blame it, but she needed to get this done.

"Problem?" Tinabella asked as Ava frowned.

"No . . ." Ava said. "I just need to find the right . . . angle."

Slowly, Ava convinced the water to do as she asked. She didn't think she could have described exactly how. It wasn't thinking about it differently, like Dorian's *two plus two equals 3:35 on a Wednesday afternoon* method. It was almost as though on some level she was having to convince herself, talk herself into the idea that she really wanted to do this.

The rope bent to the rooftop, sliding around the ten waiting poisons.

Ava had secretly worried the bottles might tip over, spilling their deadly contents too soon, but there was no need. The water kept them firmly upright without her even trying, clearly protecting itself as much as obeying her commands.

"Nice one," said Tinabella.

Ava was sweating by the time she got the bottles up to the edge of the storm.

She took a deep breath. She held it.

"Here we go . . ." she murmured.

Ava hurled the bottles forward, dropping her connection to the water a second later.

For a moment they hung suspended, glinting, barely visible.

Then the wind took them, and the world went wild.

Bursts of light blossomed on the spinning air, smearing colors across the storm: the bright fuchsia of Timmy's Complaint, Hitch-hetch's nauseating browns, Wrathspool's vinegar yellow, along with all the rest. The roaring column surged and mixed, pulling the poisons together and up, up, up, faster than Ava could follow, until, with a groan and a shift in pressure so sudden it made her ears pop, the entire storm lit up a pulsing, glaring, eye-watering electric green.

The two friends stood side by side, squinting up at the consequences of their actions.

"Um," said Ava. "I think we might have made it worse."

"Mm-hmm." Tinabella had her hands on her hips. "Guess it was a long shot that we'd get it right the first time."

"Do you think Vivienne felt that at least?" asked Ava.

"Oh yeah. There's no way that much magic wouldn't echo along the arcane resonance."

"Ha! That sounds like something from a Jonsi poem: *Echo along the arcane resonance.*"

Tinabella huffed a laugh.

They watched the storm, its constant, pulsing glare sending strange shadows rippling over Swickwit.

"Well," said Ava after a while. "Now what?"

"Now we go to bed, I guess," Tinabella said. "Then wake up and do it all over again with curses."

Ava felt a shiver of excitement. The only curses she really

knew about were Jadis's asparagus one and the one that had turned Henry from a giant into a small human-sized boy.

"And that's riskier than poisons, right?" she asked.

Tinabella nodded. "Oh yeah, since the magic has to come from us."

"I don't think I actually know how curses work," said Ava.

"I kind of do, in theory. We'll figure it out as we go."

Ava looked over at her friend, feeling a sudden urge to laugh as a giddiness rose up in her. She felt different, somehow. Older, maybe. Not like herself. Her nerves from a short while before were completely forgotten.

"Hey." She nudged Tinabella on the shoulder. "At least this is actually pretty fun."

Tinabella looked up at her, face blank. Then she smiled. "It is, Ava," she said. "Wicked fun."

20

WARDEN PIKE

Warden Pike stood in the center of the Great Hall of the Witch Council of Oz, waiting for an answer and scowling.

Shimmering blue light swirled overhead, filling the grand, round room with rainbows. The floor beneath his feet was a circle of pure gold. The walls shone with mirrors. From a balcony above, masked figures in silvery robes gazed down. More lights pulsed behind them, white and dazzling, so that it was impossible to tell how many shapes there were.

Warden Pike fought the urge to spit.

The Council had kept him waiting two days before they would see him. Two entire days and nights while every student and teacher in his charge was trapped in Vivienne Morderay's magical clutches.

Now, finally, he'd been allowed to explain why he was there and, gritting his teeth, ask the Council for help.

"That's it?" boomed one of the figures. "That is the issue for which we have been called into session?"

"Pulled from our other important duties?" added another.

"Interrupted, inconvenienced, and irked?"

The Council's voices were magically disguised, altered to sound majestic and powerful. Warden Pike thought it was all very over the top and, frankly, a little embarrassing.

"Vivienne Morderay has made your school stormy," the first councilor continued.

"And you have decided it is *our* problem?" finished another.

"With respect," called Pike, a muscle twitching in his jaw, "Dorothy's Gale is not merely *stormy*. My staff are trapped in it. I cannot get to my students." He swallowed, summoning the strength for what he had to say next. "It is magic too powerful for me. I am begging the Council for help."

Several of the councilors chuckled, and Warden Pike had to calm himself with slow, deep breaths as they put their heads together, whispering.

The Council had been formed nearly two hundred years ago in the chaos after the Wizard left, and despite his obvious power and seniority, Warden Pike had never been asked to join. Over time, he had come to accept that was just part of the cost of being head of the School for Wicked Witches. But that still didn't mean he liked it.

Who was he even talking to right now?

He squinted up at the balcony, counting six shapes—no, eight?

The heads of the four main schools had to be up there: Dean Waterwash from West Oz Witch Academy, Headmaster Mossfoot from the North, East Oz's Principal Gustbreeze, and Provost Flammis from the South.

As for the rest, there were plenty of powerful witches scattered across the land who might have won an invitation: Fiona Inish, Gordon the Oh-So-Proud, Angelíqua Woofnoof, Thrumbly Scree.

Any one of them would have enjoyed keeping him waiting, seeing him squirm, making him beg for help. These were Oz's cool witches. The popular crowd. The ones who decided who was important and excluded everyone else. Including his students.

Officially, the Council was supposed to govern the use of magic across the land, keeping truly bad witches like Vivienne Morderay, Osmuth Rust, and Filbert the Cruel in check. But did they care when it was the students at the School for Wicked Witches who were being attacked? Apparently not. The Council members cared for their own institutions well enough. But not his collection of misfits and oddballs.

The lights danced again as the councilors broke apart.

"We will consider your request," one of them called. "Please enjoy a relaxing rest as you wait."

An hour later, Warden Pike was still waiting and anything but relaxed.

Soft chimes tinkled in the rafters as he stalked from one side of the elegant foyer to the other. Sweet scents drifted through the air: jasmine and plorange and spring apple. Plants cascaded from flowering pots. Delicate art displayed idyllic scenes of Oz. A fountain burbled serenely in a corner.

None of it soothed Warden Pike.

The great golden doors suddenly cracked open, and Warden Pike spun toward the shimmering blue light in time to see a parrot come gliding out of the Great Hall.

Instantly the doors boomed closed again, leaving Warden Pike staring as the parrot flew to one of the waiting velvet sofas and settled on its back.

Scowling, he crossed the room and seated himself on the opposite end.

"Warrrden," said the parrot.

"Terry," replied Warden Pike. "What is—"

He cut off as the parrot held up a wing. It gave a loud squawk, and seconds later one of the silent mechanical guards appeared, setting a large crystal goblet of strawberry iced tea beside it. The parrot took a long, slurping drink as the guard left, and sighed.

Warden Pike eyed the bird. Terry had been the official messenger and spokes-parrot for the Witch Council since its founding, and despite their many interactions, the two of them had never become friendly. Terry's main job was to notify children with magic that they were going to magic school when they turned eleven, and Warden Pike had often wondered what the parrot got up to the rest of the year. Though he did have to admit that the bird somehow seemed to know as much about Oz as he did himself.

“Well?” said Warden Pike. “Is the Council going to help?”

The parrot ruffled its feathers. “The councilorrrs have considerrred yourrr inconvenient rrrequest, and I have been authorrrized to pass along the generrral location of Vivienne Morderrray’s lairrr.”

Warden Pike clenched his fists. “That is all? After two days of waiting?”

“The Council believes it to be morrre than fairrr.”

“How? They are offering no help. No assistance. What good is the *general location* of Vivienne’s lair without real aid?”

The parrot shrugged as it chomped down a strawberry.

“The consensus is that this is *yourrr* prrroblem, Warrrden Pike. Vivienne is one of yourrr forrrmerrr students, afterrr all. The fact that she now seems to have a vendetta against herrr old school does not affect the rrrest of Oz. Not in a way that rrrequirrres the Council to take action, at least.”

“Not a threat to the rest of Oz?” Warden Pike growled. “Vivienne has completed the Lost Collar of Arboc. Does the Council really think she will constrain herself to an old grudge against me?”

The parrot blinked, looking almost startled for a moment. Its voice was higher as it answered.

“The Council has seen no evidence Vivienne intends widerrr attacks than she has done prrreviously. If she has grrrown morrre powerrrful, that is something they will monitorrr.”

"So if I want my school back and my students and teachers restored, I have to do it myself, is that the message?" Rage was lapping at Warden Pike's ribs.

"That is the Council's forrrmal decision."

Warden Pike could have cracked the Council doors with the tension in his jaw, but he kept his composure. Over and over the witches behind those doors had set his concerns aside. Someday, he would find out exactly who he was facing in there, and what hidden agenda lurked beneath all these decisions.

"Very well." Warden Pike got to his feet. "I will take what I can get. Where, *generally*, can I find Vivienne?"

The parrot told him.

"One final question," Pike said. "Does the Witch Council of Oz care about children?"

The parrot bristled. "Prrrotecting the good people of Oz and prrromoting their well-being is ourrr highest prrriorrrity," he snapped. "Childrrren arrre included in that."

Warden Pike nodded. "Then I hope someday it will begin to care about all of them."

Turning his back on the spokes-parrot for the most powerful group of witches in Oz, he strode from the golden hall.

The winter air outside nipped at Warden Pike's ears and nose, and he almost regretted refusing the refreshments in the hall. It would be a long flight to the particular corner of North Oz the parrot had pointed him to, and he would still have to track down Vivienne once he got there.

Well, what did cold and tired and hungry matter? He would search stone by stone if he had to. He would look under every boulder, nest, and tree. The Council's attitude had made him more determined than ever. And it had also given him a new idea to consider.

If the rest of the world didn't care about outcasts like him and his students, if they wouldn't lift a finger to help, maybe Vivienne Morderay would be open to considering some kind of deal.

She was, after all, one of them.

21

STEADY STUDY PROGRESS

Two days later an ominous red 8 floated over the countdown clock in the Round Room, and the Nettle students were still wondering about the change in the storm.

Opal and Branwen thought it must be a sign Warden Pike was breaking through, but no one else did, mostly because Gern had interrogated their class about it the morning after.

"Wasn't any of my Cobweb or Cauldron lot," he'd insisted, his face more worried than ever in the green glow. "Are yeh posi'ive none of yeh tried messin' with tha' thing?"

Ava and Tinabella had both received long, searching stares, but Ava had given her best innocent face, and finally Gern let it drop, leaving Ava a little surprised at how good lying felt all of a sudden.

The growing consensus was that whatever had happened to the storm, it wasn't a threat. In a way, it was kind of pretty. The bright green light cast the whole school in a dramatic glow all day long, though everyone did have to hang blankets over their windows to be able to sleep at night.

Inside Nettle Tower, the mood was as good as it could be with the storm still in place.

Crow turned out to be a truly great leader. Even though he

was the furthest behind in every subject but juggling, he never stopped encouraging his classmates, checking on how they were doing and cheering the loudest when they leveled up and got to erase their name in the morning blackboard ritual.

They all still had plenty of learning to do, but the names on the board were definitely ticking down as Jonsi mastered color-changing illusions, Margo figured out why she'd been having trouble with light spells, and Matthew got a handle on magical plants. Crow's great idea was working.

As for Ava and Tinabella, their test preparations were going okay. Not great, not terrible, just okay. Ava had removed her name from the *History of Prophecy* list and was close to doing the same on *Astral Basics*, while Tinabella had gotten the hang of drying spells and circles of protection.

Ava knew they should have been doing better, but it was a serious challenge trying to keep up with test prep while also secretly learning how to cast and stockpile curses. She'd led a double life in the school before, back when she and Tinabella had spent every afternoon searching for a way out, but this was different. This was tough. Tinabella had been right: Compared to curses, poisons had been a piece of double-frosted bramblemallow cake.

Curses turned out to be fiercely complicated magic. They had to be layered, almost like sandwiches, with each element precisely correct for the others to work. And there were so many kinds: body curses, such as extra noses, glitter gums, or lizard scales; mind curses, like a terrible song stuck in your head or being scared of breakfast; classic curses, including bad luck and hundred-year naps; and plenty more besides. Ava knew she never would've been able to manage any of them without all the new magical theory she'd been getting from her classmates.

Little by little, she and Tinabella got the hang of the process, storing up completed curses in folded paper parcels—a trick Tinabella had discovered in her endless Punzell Tower reading—before smuggling them back to their room and piling them in the faithful laundry basket.

Ava found herself becoming fascinated by her own growing power. There was a resonance to truly wicked magic, a tone she could almost taste. It was rich and sweetly unpleasant, and left a sort of cloudy film on her mind. There was something about it she began to crave.

She even thought she smelled it sometimes in class, a rush of that same certainty of power. Once or twice it happened when she caught Tinabella's eye, and sometimes Dorian or Carmelie lifted their heads and looked over at her, their eyebrows pinched, as though she'd spoken their names.

"What have you been doing lately?" Carmelie asked over dinner one night.

"Huh?" Ava said. "What have I been doing with . . . what?"

Carmelie eyed her. "There's just this, I don't know, glamour around you now. You look better. More *you,* but in a good way."

Ava couldn't think of any response but to grin.

"Is it because of whatever you and Tinabella are up to?" Beryl asked.

Ava's grin slipped. "We're not up to anything."

Carmelie snorted. "Yeah, right. Tinabella's barely spoken to anyone else since she got back. Including me."

"And you're not hanging out with your little West Oz pal anymore," Beryl noted.

Ava spotted Henry down the table and blinked, surprised by a twinge of guilt. She'd mostly forgotten about him these past days.

"We know you're planning something," said Dorian. "Was it you two who messed up the storm?"

The perfect lie rose effortlessly to Ava's lips. "Us? How could *we* do something like that? We're not even good enough to be teaching any classes like you and Branwen and Carmelie."

"Okay, good point." Dorian nodded. "But what are you doing, then? You keep running off every afternoon. And like Carmelie said, you're both looking . . . different."

Ava's earlier pleasure at being noticed shifted into a flare of anger at having such nosy and observant classmates. Why couldn't they just take the hint?

"I really don't know," she said. "Maybe you should try not thinking about us so much." She got to her feet, picking up her tray. "Now if it's okay with you, I think I'm ready for another candleberry sundae."

With one week to go until Midwinter testing and the storm still green and raging, Ava and Tinabella had their first real mishap as they put the finishing touches on the last curses on their list.

It was midafternoon, and they were hard at work in the Swickwit gym, which had become their curse-crafting headquarters. They'd originally hoped to keep working in the greenhouse, but the cauldrons of poison they'd left there had begun to evaporate, their fumes mixing in the air in such an alarming way that all the other greenhouses had edged away from it across the courtyard.

The gym wasn't ideal, but it was free of Cobweb and Cauldron kids, and there was plenty of room to draw circles and spiky symbols on the floor, burn hair and ant milk in metal bowls, and do the necessary muttering, chanting, and yodeling without being overheard.

"Ugh, this is taking forever," Ava groaned, tying a final magical knot in a finicky little curse that would make lamps flicker annoyingly whenever someone was trying to read. "Are you sure these last few are even worth it?"

"Okay, look." Tinabella stood up from her chalk drawing of a six-armed bear, smears of bittergrass grease on her cheeks. "We've been over this: The more curses we have, the better our chances of knocking the storm out of Vivienne's control. Remember how we agreed the poison probably didn't work because ten bottles wasn't enough?"

"I know," Ava said. "But aren't some of these just pointless? The next one on my list is *Curse to make someone turn into a baked potato whenever someone says 'adventure' to them.*"

Tinabella snorted. "Well, I love that one. I found it folded up in this completely random old book on—"

"But it's got barely any power!" Ava interrupted. She wasn't sure why she was whining. She felt odd. "And it's not like we're cursing *Vivienne*. We can't go shouting 'adventure' at her the next time she attacks. We're just—"

"Disrupting the storm, I know!" Tinabella interrupted back, waving the fish-bone spoon she was holding and sending out a cascade of sparks. "And we're almost through the list, so just put your head down and finish so we can cast them all tonight!"

Tinabella was shouting, and Ava felt an answering flare of anger roll over her, leaving a quiet corner of her mind surprised at its intensity. It seemed bigger than her, like something filling the room. The air throbbed. The floor beneath them trembled. She and Tinabella held each other's eyes, and a moment later the feeling peaked, and eased, and began to ebb away.

"Um, that was weird," said Ava.

"Tell me about it." Tinabella flapped a hand, fanning

her face. "For a minute there I wanted to curse *you.*"

Ava laughed and bent back over her circle to gather components.

As she worked, she thought about the angry wave that had just swept over them. Where had it come from? They'd been getting along great since Tinabella returned. Her roommate was as bossy and opinionated as ever, but Ava had toughened up during her time at Swickwit, and she was getting better at throwing it right back. She actually thought Tinabella liked having someone push back at her, the way Carmelie did, and maybe that was the key to this new dimension of their friendship, and—

"Oh, rat cavities!"

Ava's mind had wandered, making her fumble the paper wrapper just as the baked potato curse was coming together into a glowing red splodge. She grabbed for it, missed, scuffed the edge of her chalk circle with one flailing foot, and was blasted by the releasing energy right across the room, directly into Tinabella.

"Wowch!" shouted Tinabella.

"Hwoah!" agreed Ava as Tinabella's bear drawing disintegrated and the pair of them were hurled back the other way.

Dust settled around them as they untangled themselves, groaning, and got to their feet.

"Ugh, sorry," said Ava. "I guess I got a bit distracted."

"You think?" Tinabella wore her best scowl as she brushed

doombug wings off her uniform. "Now I have to start that spell all over again."

"I said I was sorry." Ava looked around. "Do you see my curse anywhere?"

They looked. There was no sign of the glowing red lump.

"Maybe it popped?" suggested Ava.

Tinabella shook her head. "Not if you finished casting it. It probably found someone to stick to."

They looked at each other.

"Do you . . . feel cursed?" Tinabella asked.

"Um, no? You?"

"Don't think so."

"I guess we'll just have to wait and see," Ava said. "I'm kinda glad now it was only a minor one."

"And see? It was still super disruptive!" said Tinabella. "So get back to work. We're hitting Vivienne with more than she can handle tonight!"

22

THE CURSE CATASTROPHE

A strange, saturated calm filled Ava as she and Tinabella snuck out of their room and up to the Nettle Tower roof that night.

It occurred to her on the way that the two of them were getting very little sleep these days, but then they didn't seem to need it. It was almost like they were running on a second source of fuel.

Once again, they carried the laundry basket between them, though this time with Ava's old cactus dress tucked over the top—partly to hide the contents in case they ran into any classmates, and partly to keep in all the delicate paper curses if they had trouble climbing onto the roof.

It was a good thing they did. If the roots had refused to touch the basket when it was full of poison, now they actively wriggled out of the way, and even with a much lighter load, Ava and Tinabella struggled.

Finally they made it and took up their position by the spike.

The storm roared above them, the green glow even brighter by night, making the people trapped inside extra visible as their dark shapes whirled by in the wind.

"I bet they're gonna be dizzy for months once we finally

get them out of there," Ava said, nodding as the line of Broom students went whizzing past.

"Probably, but who cares?" said Tinabella, cracking her neck and stretching. "Now come on, let's show Vivienne who's really got a talent for wickedness."

Ava's calm warmed to bright anticipation as she reached out for the boiling lake again. She called up her rope of water just fine—though the lake did seem the slightest bit hesitant. But when she brought it to the roof, the whole thing coiled back on itself, refusing to come any closer.

"Um, Ava?" said Tinabella. "What are you doing?"

"I've got it," Ava said. She meant it. She'd learned from last time, and she was stronger than she'd been then. Much stronger.

Digging deep, she grabbed the water and squeezed, forcing it to pick up the basket. Something about doing it hurt somehow, but Ava was too determined to be stopped.

"Yes," Tinabella said. "Good."

The curse-filled basket surged up on its rope of boiling water, flying over the towers and rooftops to challenge Vivienne Morderay's storm.

Ava stopped it before it made contact, holding the water just beyond the wind's reach, and cackled.

"What was that for?" asked Tinabella.

A wild smile stretched across Ava's face. "I've just never felt more like a witch than I do right now."

Tinabella bared her teeth in response as her gleaming eyes met Ava's.

"Ready to make it official?" she said. "Release those curses in one . . . two—no, wait! Hang on!"

"What?" Ava huffed. "You're ruining the moment."

"Your cactus dress," explained Tinabella. "It's still on top of the basket."

"Oh. Oh yeah."

Ava gazed out at the floating shape, weighing her options. Upgraded skills or not, it was still taking most of her concentration keeping the water in line.

Obviously, she should just let the dress go. What did she need that old thing for, anyway? She never wore it. There was no point wasting time and energy bringing it back.

She became aware that something within her was fighting the idea, some fluttering pressure in the vicinity of her chest. But even as she listened, it was drowned out by a growing excitement over what she and Tinabella were about to achieve. She was about to become the girl who saved her teachers, her school, and maybe even all of Oz! The girl who beat Vivienne Morderay at her own game!

Did she really want to be the girl who rescued old laundry instead?

"Whatever," Ava said, and with one determined twist of her powers, she sent the whole basket soaring into the storm.

Tinabella whooped as the curses poured out, ripping

open in the wind, bursting like bruises in the maelstrom: purple-black, eggy orange, and sour yellow.

Ava could feel every curse she'd made going off, which had to be her first taste of arcane resonance in action. It was her magic driving them, after all. Luckily, there was none of the spinning sensation the water had given her, but as she watched, she became aware of something else, some current of familiar power resonating back to her through the link.

She leaned into the feeling, trying to catch it, but the energy kept slipping through her grasp. It was incredibly frustrating, like trying to identify someone out of the corner of your eye, made even harder because she was making this up on the spot.

Ava thought of Professor Mulch encouraging them all to get better fast, to grow, to push themselves and level up.

Well, Ava certainly had been leveling up lately. Even Carmelie had noticed.

She closed her eyes, directing her magical senses back through her curses and into the storm, twisting and grabbing in the chaos until she found that humming, tantalizing thread. It was like taming the river beside the Yellow Brick Road all over again, but ten times harder, and she tuned out everything else as she pulled, dragging herself along it, trying to get a glimpse of whatever was on the other side.

It had to be Vivienne, right?

A glow began to fill her vision, building like a light at the end of a tunnel, a fierce thrum of magic that slowly resolved, coming into focus, metallic, and golden, and—

All at once, the scars on Ava's hands zinged with a burst of energy so strong she cried out.

At the same moment, Tinabella grabbed her arm.

"Ava, open your eyes! Look!"

Ava did, and saw that the storm around them was worse. Much worse.

The wall of wind had utterly transformed wherever the curses touched it, twisting into new vortices, crackling with copper-colored lightning, or thudding with tiny explosions. One broad patch was actually on fire, orange flames roaring as they spun round and round and round.

"Well," said Ava. "I guess that didn't work."

"Mm-hmm," Tinabella said. "Not the way we wanted. It's pretty, though."

And it was, in a terrifying kind of way. Their curses had turned the storm, already glowing green and glittering, into a whirling, swirling, poisonous stained glass window.

In unison, both girls let out a delighted cackle. The coincidence made them laugh for real, which turned into a round of belly-crunching guffaws before they settled down.

"This is so fun," said Tinabella, wiping her eyes. "What were you laughing about?"

"About how this reminds me of wrecking the great hall at

West Oz Witch Academy when I did my first magic test," said Ava. "You?"

"The time I ruined the secret clock room by bringing all those animals back from North Oz."

"Oh yeah! And you were all *helllpp* and running from the bats and bears. That was hilarious!"

"Life must be so boring for other kids. They never do stuff like this."

"You're right. Poor everyone else." Ava smiled up into the tempest. "I'm almost glad it didn't work. I think I would have felt cheated if we fixed the storm just like that and never got to learn entanglement."

"It's all waiting on the scroll," Tinabella said.

"I think I almost reached Vivienne, by the way," noted Ava. "When I had my eyes closed, I followed this weird energy back to something powerful and metal. It made my scars hurt, so it was probably her."

"Seriously? That's awesome!" Tinabella eyed her. "Way to go. Maybe with entanglement you'll be able to show me, and we can take her on together."

"I've heard third time's the charm," said Ava. "Think that applies to wicked magic, too?"

Tinabella grinned, turning back for the roots, the tower, and bed.

"Only one way to find out!"

23

THE TEST PREP PARTY PLAN

All the talk over breakfast the next morning was about the seriously upgraded storm.

"It's *got* to be Vivienne Morderay," Matthew said. "I mean, lightning *and* fire?"

"Seriously," said Opal. "Maybe we should ask—hey! Jonsi!"

Jonsi appeared out of the hallway.

"Six," he said, pointing ominously at the countdown clock.

"We know," said Opal. "But did you check out the storm from your window?"

"Yes." Jonsi selected a large wool fruit from the breakfast buffet and settled onto one of the benches.

"And?" asked Wolfgang. "Did you see anything new with your magic-detecting vision?"

"Gern called it *spell-sight*," said Branwen.

Opal waved her spoon for quiet. "Jonsi, what did you see?"

Jonsi swallowed his bite of wool fruit. "The storm is full of curses now."

Ava and Tinabella, helping themselves to hootmeal and hot chocolate, locked eyes.

"Curses? Really?" said Wolfgang. "Cool!"

"What kind of curses?"

"Do you know who cast them?"

Jonsi gave a glacially slow double blink, then shook his head. "No. It looked like Vivienne at first, but the magic doesn't quite match. There is something familiar there, though. Maybe her style is changing."

"Are you positive it's not Warden Pike saving us?" asked Margo.

"Maybe?" Jonsi considered. "But if I had to bet my fingernails on it, I would say no."

"Ooh," said Opal. "It's a mystery. Unless—wait, I bet it was the older kids!"

Ava met Tinabella's eyes again, letting her relief show as the class settled into a spirited argument over whether or not the older students had been taught to cast curses.

It was certainly interesting, though, that Jonsi couldn't recognize their magic in the storm. Was it because their power was still developing? Or because the magic they'd cast was new, and advanced, and wicked? Whatever the reason, Ava was downright flattered that Jonsi had thought her and Tinabella's magic might have been Vivienne's. It was a fabulous compliment.

Once class started, Crow tried to brush off the changes in the storm and keep everyone's excitement high with their morning blackboard ritual. It almost worked, since Dorian,

Margo, and Branwen had all leveled up enough to erase their names from under another subject, and Crow, to a huge round of applause, got to erase his own name from under *History of Prophecy.*

But everything changed when Gern appeared in the open window, his huge form blocking out the stormlight as he landed on the roots with a thud.

"Hi!" said Crow. "You're, um, early, Gern. And not on the roof."

Gern nodded, holding on to the roots with his powerful arms. Most of him was still outside, and he had to duck his head to see in, his stone top hat only just clearing the gap.

"Mornin'," he said. Even from her seat, Ava spotted new worry lines on his face. He was looking positively craggy. "I know yeh've seen the storm, and I'm 'ere to say yer not to go up on the roof anymore. It's not safe."

Opal raised a hand. "So it wasn't the older students who changed it?"

Gern's head swung side to side. "No, it wasn't. To be honest, I 'aven't got a clue what's goin' on. I prob'ly shouldn't be tellin' yeh that. Plenty of other adults would prob'ly say everythin' was fine, but I believe in tellin' kids the truth. An' the truth is that storm jus' keeps gettin' worse, an' there's still no sign of Warden Pike breakin' through from outside."

Anxious murmurs filled the class.

"Swickwit's in real danger," Gern went on. "That's the

shape of it. Yeh've all done a great job focusin' on yer learnin', so please jus' keep yer 'eads down, stay inside where it's safe, an' stick to that."

From the outbreak of talk and questions, Ava could tell no one found his words reassuring.

She spotted Crow eyeing the class, his golden face pale, his bottom lip clamped between his teeth. As she watched he appeared to reach a decision, and he hurried over to Gern, leaning in and whispering.

Whatever they were discussing started with frowns and plenty of gesturing, then finished with nodding from them both.

"All right, everyone," called Gern, shouting over the noise. "Keep lookin' after each other. An' listen to Crow!"

Gern backed out the window as the class said goodbye, executing an impressive flip-turn as he kicked off the roots.

"Listen up, please!" called Crow, clapping his hands and sounding almost like Professor Mulch. "You heard Gern; let's try and focus. There's still tons of learning to be done and only six days left before the test!" He rapped his knuckles on the blackboard. "If we work together we can get every name off this list."

It was a restless, buzzy morning after that. Gern's admission that he had no idea what was going on and his warning that the storm was becoming more dangerous combined to keep everyone so easily distracted it was a wonder anyone learned anything.

Still, Beryl did finally fully leave her body in Opal's astral basics class, after days of getting stuck by her collarbone. And Jonsi and Jadis, who had already removed their names from under *Magical Plants & Fungi*, were able to help most of the group memorize the very useful "Five Leaves? Run Away!" song in Wolfgang's lesson.

Ava was still baffled by hexatic equations in mathcantations and was so annoyed when Branwen suddenly managed to do one that she began running through a mental list of curses to throw at her. It seemed the obvious course of action. She was already muttering the Dire Chant of Itchy Toenails and looking for cobwebs when a small, quiet part of her brain suggested maybe a curse wasn't exactly the thing to do just now.

Ava sat there, frowning, as two very different instincts pushed and pulled inside her. The small, quiet part won in the end, and she went back to trying to make sixteen sixes add up odd. But the pro-cursing side of her wouldn't stop muttering.

Lunch that day was zowieloaf, and noisy.

After lunch, Ava, Henry, and Tinabella were struggling through Jadis's temperature charms class when Crow popped his head into the laboratory.

"Hey, hi, hello," he said as everyone looked up and Matthew stopped balancing his fire cubes. "Can you all come back into the classroom, please? I have an announcement."

The rest of the class was already there as Ava and the others settled into their desks.

"Thanks for cutting lessons short," said Crow, bouncing on his toes beside the blackboard. "I know you're all looking forward to whatever you've got planned for the afternoon, but I think you'll be more excited about this. Some of you probably saw me talking with Gern this morning, and I wanted to tell you that with his blessing, we're, well, we're having a party!"

For a moment no one spoke, then Carmelie guffawed.

"A party? Here?! When has there ever been a party at Swickwit?"

"Actually," said Crow, "they throw one at the end of every year. One for each level. For Nettle it's a graduation, so I've missed it two times now. But I hear it from my room and see the mess after. It's got food and music and decorations and everything."

"But this isn't the end of the year!" Beryl said.

"And none of us are graduating," called Dorian.

Crow held up his hands. "I know, I know. But I saw how stressed and worried everyone looked this morning. You've all been working super hard! So I checked with Gern, and he said since he's technically the head of the school right now, he can pull a few strings, and, well . . . we're having our party tonight!"

The morning's restlessness erupted into gleeful enthusiasm, complete with cheering and colored sparks going off like fireworks. Branwen even conjured up a crowd of her shadow bunnies to do a celebratory dance around the classroom.

"And everyone gets to help get ready," Crow called over the noise. "The food and stuff will show up on its own later, but we have to decide what kind of party we want it to be ourselves."

More cheers greeted this announcement. Ava and Tinabella didn't join in.

"This is the worst!" Tinabella grumbled into Ava's ear. "We've got important entanglement research to do! Do you think we should curse everyone so they all hate having fun? Or poison them, maybe? They can't throw a party when they're puking."

Ava eyed her whooping classmates, considering. "I actually think we deserve a party more than anyone else," she said. "We're doing twice as much work. And you heard Gern: There's no sign of Warden Pike breaking through the storm anytime soon. How about we take a break and have fun with this, then work extra hard tomorrow?"

"Huh!" Tinabella tilted her head, then nodded. "You're right, we do deserve a party. So long as it's a really good one."

"Have you been to a good one before?" Ava asked.

"So many. My dad may be awful, but he's super rich,

remember? I used to go to tons of fancy events, with a fancy outfit on, and fancy jewels and fancy drinks and dancing and all of it."

For a moment the shimmer in Ava's mind cleared, and a memory of her large, noisy family's homemade birthday celebrations—which certainly did *not* include fancy outfits and jewels—filled her vision. She saw the gift bowl with its tea towel covering to hide the surprise (even though everyone always got a new pair of homemade socks). She saw her brothers and sisters singing the "Now You Are Older, Now Older Are You" song. She saw her pet miniature tortoise, Peaches, scavenging under the table for crumbs of rose cactus cake.

How strange. She hadn't thought about her family in a while.

"Hello? Ava?" Tinabella snapped her fingers. "Where'd you go?"

Ava shook her head. "Sorry! I was just—I don't think I've ever been to a party. Not a really good one."

"Well, get ready," said Tinabella. "They're a lot of work, but they are so worth it."

The first thing the class did to prepare for their party was vote on a theme. Jadis's zombie funeral idea didn't get a single vote apart from hers, though it did get some worried glances. Henry's idea for a pajama party got a little more support, and almost half the class liked Dorian's suggestion of the night sky.

In the end it was Branwen who came up with the Emerald City theme. Everyone knew about the Emerald City: It was where all the wealthiest people in Oz lived, and everything was supposedly green and fancy and fashionable and amazing. The fact that none of them had ever actually visited turned out to be an advantage, since it meant they could just make up whatever they wanted, and with the storm already turning all of Swickwit green, the idea was a hit.

"Listen up!" announced Tinabella, climbing onto her desk once the unanimous approval had passed. "We need to break into teams to get this done right. Trust me, I know. I want four people on decorations with me, and the rest of you split up into games, music, and food."

"The food's covered," called Crow. "We don't get a say in that."

Tinabella rolled her eyes. "Fine! Then split up into decorations, games, music, and helpers!"

Possibly because it was the most Tinabella had spoken to the others since she'd gotten back, everyone jumped to follow her instructions. Ava ended up as a general helper with Matthew and Opal, and Tinabella immediately sent them off to find a supply of opera ivy while she showed her team the decorating charm she'd used on their dorm room.

It took a bit longer than expected to track down the

ivy—they finally spotted it coiled around a chandelier, serenading the empty theater—and when Ava, Matthew, and Opal got back, they found the Round Room, classroom, and hallway fully decked out in Emerald City décor.

Tinabella's decorating charm had worked wonders. The walls were green velvet patterned with diamonds; the floor was a perfect, shining sheet of lime marble; portraits of extremely fancy Ozians hung here and there, all made up by whoever cast the spell, but looking very realistic; and little chairs and tables crowded with useless but expensive-looking gold and crystal knickknacks clustered in every corner.

Jadis had insisted on decorating the laboratory by herself, and the results, while exciting, were also a bit worrying, given the ceiling-high mountain of jade paper chains exploding out of the pillow fort and the green sports socks shoved over every one of the bottles.

Crow was on a ladder, busy hanging glittering avocado lights, and Ava spotted Henry helping to assemble a set of South Oz splash cymbals.

She felt a happy shiver of anticipation. After spending so much time in Nettle Tower since school started, it was thrilling to see it looking so different.

The afternoon flew by, and there was always something to do, from stacking the classroom desks out of the way with Carmelie, to helping Beryl transfer a library map of the Emerald City onto the hallway ceiling, to pulling the warbling opera ivy out of Dorian's tuba again. Tinabella seemed to be everywhere, shouting instructions and pointing out mistakes, but it all added to the festive mood, and no one appeared to mind.

At last, the preparations were done, and everyone went back to their rooms to get changed. They all waited anxiously, nerves high and stomachs growling, until, at a signal from Crow echoing down the hall, the party of Nettle Tower began.

24

THE PARTY

Looking back on it later, Ava realized her very first non-family party had been pretty much perfect.

She and Tinabella took their time getting ready. With no fancy clothes of her own, plus no party experience, Ava allowed Tinabella to dress her for the occasion. This was tricky at first, since Tinabella was shorter, but her solution—draping Ava in all the black fabric she could find—seemed to work fine. Tinabella wore an embroidered high-collared jacket and pants in deepest purple, and standing side by side, Ava thought they must look wicked enough for any celebration.

They were the last to arrive in the Round Room, and the party was already starting. They stopped in the doorway, taking in the scene.

Their chattering classmates were decked out in fancy outfits from all across Oz, which meant everything from chain mail capes to puffy silk sleeves to paper-bag jumpsuits. Added to the decorations and the green firefly lights dancing overhead, it made the familiar Round Room appear just as Ava imagined the Emerald City must be: exquisite, strange, and intoxicating.

"You two look so cool!" Henry said, coming over. "But why

aren't you wearing your cactus dress, Ava?" Henry wore a fancy frilled suit with a wide blue sash and plenty of ribbons and bows. Ava recognized it as a smaller version of the uniform she'd seen his parents wearing all those months ago at West Oz Witch Academy.

"My what?" Ava said.

Henry blinked. "Your cactus dress? The one your dad made for you? You wore it on the first day back at WOW, and the day we escaped."

"Oh," Ava said, "that." For some reason she was having trouble picturing the garment. "I guess I got rid of it sometime."

"Really?" Henry's eyes widened.

"Sure. Why would I keep it?"

"Come on," said Tinabella, tugging at Ava's elbow. "Food time. I'm hungry."

Since the school was taking care of the food, Ava had been expecting a slightly fancier version of their dining hall meals. But one glance at the groaning table taking up an entire side of the Round Room told her she was wrong.

There were ostridon steaks, fried hatchfish, crackle chips, hotroot salad, crispy thwips, mashed rumtums, buttercomb pudding, brambleberry candies, toasted crunch munch, sour leeches, glowbubbles, star sandwiches, and ploranges—and those were just the dishes Ava recognized. The Nettle kids fell on it all like wolves.

The more they ate, the more food there seemed to be, and

after curing the worst of their hunger pangs, everyone turned their attention to having the most fun possible.

Just as with their clothes, having kids from all across Oz meant there were plenty of games to learn and share. Opal was a natural at Oot Oot Derby, which left all the North Oz kids grumbling, and Matthew taught everyone Wall Smash, which mostly involved sprinting from one side of the room to the other and laughing. Ava felt a flicker near her heart as she watched her classmates, reminded for the tiniest moment of sand-quake, and her family. Then it was gone, and she started enjoying herself again.

Tinabella turned out to be a terror at Carmelie's favorite game, Monochrome. Ava spotted her cheating with a prism spell, but didn't say anything. Magic was magic, so what did it matter?

They made up their own games, too. Margo organized a race between Branwen's shadow bunnies and Beryl's creepy ceramic dolls; Wolfgang came up with a genuinely dangerous mishmash of flying sparks and hopscotch; and Dorian had a real hit when he invented Who Me?, where he randomly swapped around the whole class's faces and everyone tried to guess whose they had first.

The games weren't the only thing keeping the party grooving, of course. All the instruments Tinabella had ordered were piled on one of the benches, and each of them got pulled out and played throughout the night with varying degrees of skill. Luckily, a few people knew some simple melody charms, and Ava got to see how kids from far and wide stamped, pranced, and strutted to more kinds of music than she'd known existed. Jonsi turned out to be king of the dancing, and when his North Oz ice stomp really got going, every single one of them joined in.

The party ebbed and flowed as time burned along and the winter evening gave way to real, *staying up late* night. Spell contests replaced the dancing. A dent began to appear in the food. Ava kept losing Tinabella and finding her again, both of them breaking into helpless cackles on one occasion when Wolfgang, eyeing them side by side, asked if they were dressed up as Wicked Mode. Henry's suit was a hit. Crow seemed to be everywhere at once, encouraging the revels, making sure everyone was having fun.

The party center kept moving around, shifting with the social tides from the Round Room to the classroom to the lab. Strange cliques and mini side groups formed and broke apart. At one point Ava found herself sitting among the roots in the classroom window with Carmelie and Margo, the three of them making up a hilariously weird song about what the different colors in the storm would smell like. Half an hour later she was standing on one of the Round Room benches with Jadis's arm around her shoulder, cheering on Branwen in a glitter-catching contest as the whole class shouted themselves hoarse.

It was, all in all, a pretty great party.

* * *

At last most of the food was gone, the decorations were ruined, the green firefly lights were failing, and the mood at the top of Nettle Tower shifted toward bed.

Tinabella and Ava were among the first to leave, waving vaguely over their shoulders as they headed down the hall, yawning.

Ava was glad to change into her pajamas back in their room. The black-draped costume had been fun, like getting to be someone else for a night, but it was a relief returning to something less dramatic.

Flopping onto her bed, she reached over to her desk for Tinabella's revenge scroll. It was becoming quite battered: torn in three places and splattered with wax, stains, and assorted fruit juices from all their poison brewing and curse construction.

Ava unrolled it to the *Entanglement* section and scanned Tinabella's notes, marveling at how many details, codes, and tricks there were to learn in magic.

"This entanglement stuff is seriously complicated," she said as Tinabella emerged from the bathroom in her pajamas. "I'm glad we took a break for the party, but we've got so much to do starting tomorrow."

"I know," Tinabella said. "It was a nightmare copying it all down. We'll figure it out in the end, though. We always do."

The last sounds of excited kids and slamming doors

echoed outside as Ava returned the scroll to her desk, Tinabella checked the curtain blocking out the storm, and the two of them climbed into bed.

Ava stared into the darkness, thinking.

It had been a marvelous night. And a strange one. The wicked glow inside her had gone quiet at the party, uncertain what to make of the total departure from her normal school life and confused by the chaotic blend of competition, friendship, and fun.

Happily, she could already feel it returning.

Tinabella was right, the greedy glow told her. They would figure out entanglement. They would take down the storm. They would defeat Vivienne Morderay in the end.

Ava rolled over and smiled, snuggling into her pillow.

The end couldn't come soon enough.

25

THE ENTANGLEMENT TANGLE

Two days seemed to be the sweet spot for learning wicked magic, because it took Ava and Tinabella exactly that long to master the basics of entanglement.

Crow's party plan had been an incredible success, and after setting the tower back to normal, the Nettle students were attacking their studies with more vigor than ever before.

The social dynamics had shifted, too. Everyone was still impressed with Jonsi for his epic dancing and Margo for her terrifying flügelhorn performance. Jadis still wasn't speaking to Beryl over the pickle incident, but Beryl was only just getting her voice back after the monster-screaming contest, so it didn't much matter.

All the Nettle students shared a new energy now, as though the party had let off years of steam. Ava and Tinabella felt it, too, each of them abruptly leveling up in most of their remaining classes, though they couldn't have said how they did it. The more they buried themselves in their studies of entanglement, the less they cared about anything else. Every moment was obscured by the shimmery glow of their secret new obsession, because entanglement, it turned out, was *seriously* wicked.

Entanglement was like poison and curses combined,

capturing its victim both inside and out. Its magic was based on a core belief that you were better than the person you were entangling, that you had the right to make choices for them, to shove them aside.

It was also incredibly difficult to learn, even with the intricate charts, graphs, sigils, and notes Tinabella had copied down on the scroll. Fortunately, they had a perfect starting place to work from, since Tinabella had recently been entangled by a soup cookbook.

"Or maybe it was the other way round," she said, sketching jinx charts on a piece of parchment. "I still can't tell. But the point is, the spell that got me stuck inside that book is super similar to all this entanglement stuff. If I'd known more wicked magic, it might have even worked."

Ava erased the mathcantation she was working on and started again. "I've been meaning to ask," she said. "What was your plan for getting out of the book again if you escaped Punzell Tower?"

"Burdock. I figured he'd be able to spot me in there and get me out."

Ava looked over in surprise. "That's kind of a big risk."

"So?" Tinabella's pen scratched across the page. "I was not about to be trapped in there for one more boring day!"

With the end of the *Revenge on Vivienne* project in sight, Ava and Tinabella worked harder than ever before, building their knowledge in every free minute and staying up late into the night. Things really came together when they decided to try adding group magic to the mix. It would offer limited results with just the two of them, but should still add up to more magical force than they each had working alone.

Ava got her first taste of Tinabella's magic as they group-worked a simple conjuring spell for practice. To her surprise, it felt cool, dry, dense, and surprisingly soft, like deep moss over stone, though there was also a web of fiery, unshakable certainty crackling through it. Ava—who thought she'd known her roommate pretty well—was a little intimidated at first, but then their conjuring went so well their dorm room was briefly the most haunted place in Swickwit, and her confidence returned with interest.

They were going to entangle that storm with everything they had. They were going to shatter Vivienne's hold.

This time, it was absolutely going to work.

As the third day after the party ended, with the clock in the Round Room glowing a violet 3 and the rest of their classmates drifting off to bed, Ava and Tinabella looked up from the last lines of the scroll and agreed: They were as ready as they could be.

It was time for their best and final attempt to out-wicked Vivienne Morderay and her storm.

Ava and Tinabella's door gave a low, ominous groan as they tiptoed into the hall.

"Ha! Even our door's going wicked!" Ava whispered. Tinabella shushed her.

A moment later, they both froze at a cough from Matthew and Jonsi's room. Ten long, heart-thudding seconds passed, but after no further noise, they pressed silently on.

The Round Room was quiet and empty, and as they closed the hallway door behind them, the 3 above the countdown clock shimmered and vanished, replaced by a glowing, tangerine 2.

Ava gave the clock a jaunty wave as they passed. She felt fabulous. What had Carmelie said the other day? That there was a glamour around her now? Everyone seemed to have noticed it at the party, and tonight she could feel it. She felt like an unstoppable wave. She felt like a dune lion hunting. She was finally becoming the important, powerful witch she'd always dreamed of being.

There was no need for the faithful laundry basket tonight, no bottles or folded paper curses to lug along with them. Ava had thought that would make getting up onto the roof a breeze, but as she and Tinabella climbed out the classroom window, the roots went into open rebellion.

"What's wrong with these things?" asked Tinabella, digging in her nails as her handholds bucked and twisted.

"Hey! Easy!" Ava yelped at the roots. "It's us! Remember? The saviors of Nettle Tower?"

"And the whole entire school?" added Tinabella.

"Right! So be nice!"

The climb went a little smoother after that, just enough for the two girls to clamber up and over and across the roof to the spike.

They stood side by side, each taking in the wild green glow of the storm shimmering with fire, lightning, and the pulsing bruises of their curses.

Ava thought it looked absolutely beautiful. She could feel the churning tension of all that wicked magic making its mark on the world.

"It's funny thinking about our first night up here," said Tinabella. "Remember?"

Ava laughed. "We tried to poison the storm away from Vivienne."

"So foolish," Tinabella said. They shared a look, the velvety, bittersweet burr of wickedness flaring between them.

"Ready?" asked Ava.

Tinabella rolled her shoulders. "Let's do this."

They stood back-to-back. In unison, they reached out, folding their magic together, each one anchoring the other, letting their power build along with their shared determination to beat Vivienne, to wrench the storm from her control, to rattle the threads of arcane resonance so hard the wicked witch's red lacquered teeth would shake. To get their grand, important, *famous for the rest of our lives* revenge.

Wicked magic shimmered around them, coming *from*

them now, young and hungry, as they traced the mental and magical path toward entanglement. It felt incredible.

With a tap of Tinabella's fingers on Ava's wrist, they reached out together for the storm.

The impact was world-ending.

Ava split in two, half her mind pulled into the pummeling wind, half left reeling in her body. She flailed, grasping for a mental handhold, a single second of calm to understand what in the Nettle Smith's name had happened.

Above them, the center of the cyclone erupted, boiling over with smoke-black clouds as a vortex formed within the vortex and molten-red sparks began drifting down.

Ava's body heard the sparks settling on the school, felt them nip at her skin, smelled them burn her robes and hair, all while half her awareness was caught in the green-swirling dizziness of the storm, slashed by curses and broken glass and poison as she spun and spun and spun.

She fought against it all, trying everything she'd learned from practicing entanglement, crafting curses, brewing poison, even studying with her classmates for the Midwinter tests, as Tinabella did the same behind her, their blended magic pushing and pulling.

But the storm held them tight.

Desperate, Ava tried and failed to reach out for the lake. She called on whatever magic lay in the scars in her hands. She hurled every curse fragment she could remember. She opened her mind to claw through the gale, searching for the thread from last time leading back to Vivienne.

All she found was chaos and the sheer insignificance of her own wicked magic.

If she had still had a voice, she would have laughed. She and Tinabella had never stood a chance. Not a flicker of hope. For the first time she understood the unstoppable power of the thing that had been set around her school.

They hadn't disrupted Vivienne's hold on the storm at all.

All they'd done, once again, was make it stronger.

A furious roar broke through Ava's despair, and suddenly there was Gern, flying out of the fortress, his stone body stained bloodred and purple-green in the awful light, anger clear on his face as he charged into the new vortex of smoke and cinders.

The gargoyle shouted something Ava couldn't make out, and a shield of golden threads appeared around him, glowing like the sun they hadn't seen for days as his hands began pulling ropes of spring-green light from thin air, binding them together into a spear.

He looked magnificent, and Ava's heart leapt as he sped toward the center of the storm. She braced herself for a clash, a flare of light, a triumphant shout of victory . . .

The storm swallowed Gern whole.

Thunder rumbled like deep laughter through the smoke-dark clouds.

The gale kept on spinning.

Grief and shock hammered at Ava like physical blows. He couldn't be lost! Not Gern! She thought of his smile, his top hat, his patient exasperation with her and the boys every time they got into trouble, his confusing accent, his new eye wrinkles, his laugh.

Amid the layers of chaos and magic wrapping around her, Ava felt her heart wake up.

Suddenly, all she wanted in the world was to be back inside. Forget trying to get the best of Vivienne, forget revenge, forget becoming powerful and famous and important by taking down the storm. They had failed, and now Gern was trapped, too.

She sensed a similar change in Tinabella, and they pulled against the storm together, heaving their magic away from the maelstrom.

Little by little, it worked, and Ava felt something being left behind on the poisoned wind as she rejoined her body. It was sweet and glossy, and refused to be parted from Vivienne's magic, which meant whatever it was, Ava didn't want it. She felt it peel off her until, like the snapping of a rope, the spinning in her head stopped and she found herself back all in one piece on the roof.

Ava collapsed onto her hands and knees, panting as though she'd sprinted up every step of Nettle Tower. She heard Tinabella stagger behind her, and they both instinctively dropped their magic, wrapping their arms protectively around themselves. Ava had never felt so happy to be small, contained, and simply and only herself.

"Disaster," Tinabella croaked.

Ava tried to speak, but there was ash in her throat, and she could only nod.

Shivering in spite of the sparks and the sweat beading their foreheads, Ava and Tinabella helped each other across the roof of Nettle Tower. The roots were calm once more, easy to navigate, and they were soon back inside, out of the chaos.

They slid to the stone floor of the classroom, trembling with shock.

Tinabella spoke first. "Was that . . . as bad as I think it was?"

Ava nodded. Everything had changed. She felt as though she'd been caught in a dream this past week, and now she was wide awake again.

What had they been *doing*? What had *she* been doing, messing with wicked magic, and ignoring the boys, and . . .

"My dress!" Ava choked out, remembering. "I fed my cactus dress to the storm!"

Tinabella let out a groan.

"So much for revenge."

"So much for being famous and important."

"We really messed up."

"You've got that right!" said a voice.

Abruptly, the classroom was alive with lights, and the shadows at the back of the room were swept aside to reveal a wall of green pajamas, crossed arms, and outraged expressions.

Every single one of their classmates was awake and waiting for them.

"You two," said Carmelie, stepping forward, "have some major explaining to do."

26

VIVIENNE

Vivienne Morderay huffed in gorgeous and supreme annoyance.

Why did good things always have to end so soon?

Her growing boredom now that she was all-powerful had been cut in half since someone inside Swickwit started messing with her storm. But now it looked like that might be over. At least for a while.

She'd been harvesting crystal slugs by moonlight when the first surprise came. At first she'd thought it was an attack on her lair, but then she got her magical senses sorted out and realized someone was trying to poison her storm. She couldn't remember when she'd laughed so hard. The Dorothy Gale was like Vivienne herself now: immune to all wickedness.

The poison only made the storm stronger, and Vivienne had a marvelous time all the next day picturing the dismay of whichever Cobweb or Cauldron students had made the attempt. It had to have been them, she reasoned, with the teachers and Broom students already caught in her net. And Warden Pike knew better, of course. Even Gern the gargly-goyle wouldn't attempt something as rough and direct as poison.

She did wonder about Warden Pike, though. Why hadn't she sensed his magic yet? Why hadn't he tried to fight her off?

Still, it made her happy knowing someone was doing *real* wicked magic at Swickwit again. Poison was cliché, but it was a start, and she was proud of whoever was taking the first steps down the path she herself had followed a hundred years before.

Vivienne moved to the window, remembering how her self-education in true wickedness had landed her in trouble time and time again. Brilliant, driven, and free from silly moral constraints, she had earned herself more than a few weeks in the lonely comfort of Punzell Tower.

It was a ridiculous way to deal with wickedness, of course. She'd always thought so. All Punzell Tower had done was focus her vision—and provide the inspiration for her current lair. There really was nothing like an enormously high tower with killer views, somewhere she could look down on the world below, free from all company but the wind and the passing birds.

The second incident a few days later had been even more interesting. Vivienne had been dozing on her canopied bed when the thread between her and the storm began to twang. Someone was releasing new magic into the pattern, and it was acting like oil on flame.

"Curses!" Vivienne had shouted, sitting up. She'd laughed

again, since the curses in question were weak, almost comic. They practically tickled.

Then something unexpected had happened: She had felt a presence. Some small magical talent had managed to follow the thread anchoring her to the gale. Vivienne had sat very still in her satin sheets, the night and stars and darkness all around her as the presence approached.

Once when she was seven or eight, before magic found her, Vivienne wandered away from the carnival she'd been raised in. They were camped on the edge of Gillbreth Forest, and Vivienne had been sitting under a tree, dreaming of a bigger, more fabulous life, when there was a rustling of leaves and a liquid-silver unicorn appeared out of the gloom.

Liquid-silver unicorns didn't approach people, ever, and Vivienne had sat frozen, barely breathing, tears of delight running down her face as the gorgeous creature stepped delicately forward and touched its velvet nose to her hand.

Of course, that was when the fireworks went off back at the tents. A pattering of crystal hooves, and she was alone again.

No one had ever believed her about the unicorn. Her father had even punished her for lying, sending her to scrub out the caramel-apple buckets. But Vivienne had never forgotten that moment of breathless waiting.

She'd felt just like that as the small, strange presence approached through the storm.

For one moment it had become clear, and she saw the face of a young girl. Not the hard, fiery one who had given her the book and begged to become her apprentice. The other one. The talented one.

But this girl was in Nettle! Only eleven years old, or twelve at the most!

Vivienne had watched her as the girl stared, apparently transfixed by the thread leading to the Lost Collar of Arboc. Then the girl was gone, vanishing as quickly as the unicorn, leaving Vivienne alone, blinking and wondering.

Suddenly, she had understood.

The girl was changing her mind! The unbeatable power of the storm had impressed her, and she had been showing off her best wicked magic in hopes of earning a second chance to take her place at Vivienne's side.

What other reason could there be?

After that, Vivienne had waited, impatient and curious to see what magic the girl would try next. And tonight it had finally happened.

Oh, what a payoff it had been!

She'd been enjoying a late snack of grayberry cakes dipped in hot tea, aware now that her little fan in Swickwit always made her offerings around midnight. She'd smiled as she'd chewed, remembering her own nighttime escapades around that castle, then literally fallen off her chair as the world suddenly split in two.

Stumbling to her feet, every feather on her head bristling, she tuned in to her inner sight, soaring as fast as thought back along the magic to her beautiful, perfect storm, where she stopped in utter disbelief.

Entanglement.

The silly girl—no, both silly girls this time, judging by the joined magic—were trying to *entangle* the storm. What. Were. They. Thinking?

Vivienne couldn't even laugh as the two of them writhed, the wicked halves they'd so carefully cultivated stuck like ants in glue in the spellweave of the cyclone.

The girl who'd brought her the book was putting up a frankly impressive struggle, but Vivienne's girl, her possible apprentice, sadly seemed to be losing confidence with every spin.

And as for the storm—what a reaction! This was beyond anything Vivienne had expected, some transmutation not mentioned once in *Volatilium Gemmis*. She would have to add her own notes in the margins.

Vivienne leaned dramatically against the table, lost in the magical link as she savored the chaos over Swickwit, the smoky tang of the supercharged storm, and the brave desperation of her girls. Maybe they were both worth considering, after all. Or maybe she should make them fight it out for her attention! May the best apprentice win.

But the surprises weren't over, because suddenly Gern

was there, charging like the great granite fool he was into the heart of the storm.

Vivienne's cackle cracked through her lair, startling the dozing mustard bird in its golden cage.

The gargly-goyle was trying to use his magic to dislodge her. Gargly-goyle magic was powerful, true—she could feel its zing from here, fresh and green—but she was stronger. Her storm was stronger. And it swallowed Gern just like the rest.

For some reason this seemed to upset the girls. Vivienne frowned. Why were they struggling like that? They should be proud! And grateful, too, to have one less grown-up cramping their style at school.

But there they went, twisting out of the storm, leaving a serious chunk of their wicked magic behind.

Vivienne sighed. It would take time for them to rebuild all that. What a shame.

It was all over far too soon, and now here she was, the excitement done, gorgeously bored again.

A rough squawk came from behind her, and she turned to glare at the bird. Was she to have no peace? Couldn't the horrible thing see she was brooding?

The bird squawked louder, flapping its wings, gesturing with its head toward the northern window. Vivienne turned to look.

Another mustard bird sat on the window ledge, its

feathers ruffling in the wind, its flat white eyes reflecting the glow of her platinum lamps.

"Huh!" Vivienne huffed a laugh, then waved her hand. For a moment there was a strange resistance, and the collar grew warm around her neck. Then the watching bird was inside the cage beside the first one.

The new bird panicked, beating its wings, scrabbling at the bars, sending the golden cage swinging until it seemed to accept its fate and settled down into a sullen, icy stillness.

"Wise," Vivienne said to it. "Ask your friend there how easy it is tooo escape from Vivienne Morderay." She preened her own mane of lustrous black feathers. "Don't worry, I won't keep youuu locked in there long. Now that I've got twooo of youuu, I'm thinking a cape. Or possibly earrings. Won't that be grand?"

The birds watched her, grave and silent.

Vivienne turned to gaze out the window, slipping comfortably back into her dreadful mood.

Why did the gargly-goyle have to be defeated so easily? Why couldn't he have put up a real fight?

Where was the fun in being all-powerful if no one would challenge her?

At least she had her prospective apprentices working hard to win her favor.

Hopefully, it wouldn't take too long for their next attempt.

And hopefully they would help bring her the one big prize still missing from her collection: Warden Threnody Pike.

27

WARDEN PIKE

Warden Threnody Pike was utterly furious with himself.

Of all the things he'd done in his long, long life, getting captured by Vivienne Morderay and shoved into a birdcage was by far the most embarrassing.

It had taken days to track down Vivienne's lair using Terry the parrot's directions. Day after day of gliding over forests and hills and mountains, searching every rock and bone for flickers of magic. In the end it was a faint thread of perfume that had shown him the way, a trace of lilac out of place in the snowy heights, and despite Vivienne's best efforts, Warden Pike had succeeded, landing right on her window ledge.

That was when things went wrong, because her lair had been completely distracting. Warden Pike's bird-form brain had been dazzled by all the shininess, even as the human part of him wondered how anyone could possibly need that many bejeweled lamps or crystal mirrors or fur-trimmed rose-gold coasters.

He'd been so busy gawking he hadn't seen the bird gesturing his way until it was too late. Vivienne had turned, and by Lurline, her spellwork had grown fast!

There had been a shockingly brief battle as he'd tried to

transform, and next moment he'd found himself captured and locked in this cage.

Well, at least he'd be able to keep an eye on her now.

For all the good it would do.

The hum in his claws told him the cage was a simple but highly effective conjuring blocking any and all magic. No transforming for him, then; no speaking, no fighting Vivienne, no interfering with her plans. He couldn't even bring up the option of making a deal. Until she let him out, he was well and truly trapped. And might be on his way to a new life as an earring.

It was a large cage, with room for half a dozen birds, and there was space for the two trapped creatures to examine each other warily.

Vivienne had clearly taken out her boredom on the first mustard bird, judging by its bright purple plumage awash with fuchsia zigzags. Apart from that, it looked perfectly ordinary to Warden Pike, one more common inhabitant of North Oz's lonely hills and mountains.

Then their eyes met, and both birds froze.

Warden Pike had seen his own flat white gaze reflecting back at him earlier in the window. Now he was staring into one bright orange eye and one silvery, branching scar.

The bird let out a soft chuckle.

The orange eye winked. Twice.

Warden Pike tossed his head, displaying as much

irritation as he could in his feathered form, and firmly turned his back.

It was bad enough he'd been captured by a former student. Bad enough he had no choice now but to wait for Vivienne to mess up and grant him a chance to escape. Bad enough his school was trapped in the grip of terrifyingly strong wicked magic.

But being stuck in a birdcage with Osmuth Rust?

That was just adding insult to injury.

28

A GROUP DECISION

Ava couldn't remember ever being more exhausted.

The energy that had been driving her for days had evaporated, left behind in the storm, and all her late nights and long days studying wicked magic seemed to come crashing down at once. All she wanted in the world was to stumble back to her bed and go to sleep.

But the wall of angry classmates standing in front of her had other ideas.

Their faces were hard to look at—angry, confused, and frightened. Worst of all were Henry, looking baffled and betrayed under his pink hair, and Crow, whose open, honest face couldn't hide his hurt and disappointment.

Margo was livid. "It *was* you, this whole time! You've been lying to all of us! And to Gern!"

"He's gonna be so mad when he finds out!" said Beryl.

Ava's stomach swooped, and she and Tinabella shared a guilty glance.

"What?" demanded Wolfgang.

Ava told them.

"You lost Gern?!" Margo shouted. Opal covered her face with her hands. Matthew looked sick.

"We didn't *lose* him," insisted Tinabella. "He just showed up and decided to finally attack the storm, I guess."

"After you two made it even worse," said Carmelie.

"He probably thought he had no other choice," Beryl pointed out. "So it totally *is* your fault."

Crow seemed more worried than angry. "What were you doing, anyway?" he asked. "I get that you were probably trying to stop the wind, but . . . why? What made you think you could handle it all on your own?"

Ava's nerves were getting the better of her, and as she opened her mouth to answer, an old, unstoppable reaction bubbled up instead.

"This is no time to be laughing," said Jadis. "It's not funny."

Ava nodded, agreeing but unable to stop the giggles pouring out of her. It was wrong and awkward and totally embarrassing, but knowing that just made her laugh harder.

"Yeah, we were taking on the storm," Tinabella answered, shooting a deeply annoyed look at Ava. She summarized the revenge plan she'd developed in detention, and arcane resonance, and how she and Ava had been learning wicked magic in secret to try to tackle the storm head-on.

By the time she finished, Ava's laughter was dissipating enough for her to watch her classmates' reactions.

Margo couldn't stop shaking her head. Beryl glared. Dorian and Jadis just seemed flabbergasted. Henry looked like he was trying not to cry.

"Okay, this is a lot," Crow said, rubbing a hand over his face. "And it's late. I think we should all go to bed for now. We can decide what to do in the morning."

With some grumbles and many looks aimed at Tinabella and Ava, the group broke up, drifting back toward their rooms.

To Ava's surprise, Carmelie stuck around, weaving through the desks toward them. She stopped, peering out the window at the sparks still raining down from the storm, then held out a hand.

"You look like you again," she said, helping Ava to her feet. "Normal you."

Ava grimaced. "We're not glamorous anymore?"

"Definitely not." Carmelie looked between her and Tinabella. "But I'm still impressed."

"Hey, let's go," called Crow from the doorway. "Bed."

The three girls shared a look, all of them suppressing small smiles, and amid the exhaustion and chaos and worry, Ava felt a tiny happy curl in her stomach.

"Next time, though," Carmelie whispered, leading the way back across the classroom, "you better count me in!"

Breakfast the next morning was incredible, as though the school could tell the Nettle students needed a boost. The table in the center of the Round Room was crowded with buttercomb pancakes, mashroot meringues, sliced clearfruit, puzzle pies, and so much more, with the glowing 2 on the countdown clock shining over it all.

Sadly, the happy vibes stopped there. The changes to the storm outside looked even worse by daylight, and an anxious pall settled over the group as the day got started.

They were truly and totally on their own now. There were the older students, of course, but they wouldn't so much as look at the Nettle kids. There was Burdock, but he was confined to the library. There was the school itself, but whatever ancient magic kept it cleaning up and feeding them and restocking their soap and toothpaste wasn't a person, an authority figure, someone they could talk to and count on.

Ava and Tinabella were the last to arrive at breakfast, both with dark circles under their eyes.

The class muttered as they entered the Round Room and whispered as they got food. All the benches were full, so they sat on the floor in front of the laboratory.

To Ava's relief, Carmelie left her bench to come sit beside Tinabella. She was even more grateful when Henry did the same a moment later, grabbing two steaming mugs of hot chocolate on the way and dropping down on Ava's right.

"Hi," he said, handing her one of the mugs.

"Oh, Henry." Ava felt a prickling at the back of her eyes. "Thank you."

Crow, who was camped across the room next to Branwen, got to his feet. The room went quiet.

"Morning, everyone," he said. "Now we're all here, I thought maybe instead of class, we should start today with a bit of a chat."

The tension in the room ratcheted up. Ava gulped.

"Ugh," groaned Dorian. "Does this mean we're going to talk about *them* again?" He waved a slice of clearfruit at Tinabella and Ava. "We're *supposed* to be focusing on the Midwinter tests, but oh no, those two have to keep sneaking around and making the whole world weirder for everyone!"

"Hey, there's always weirdness in this place," huffed Tinabella. "It's not our fault we keep getting caught in it."

"No, you're wrong!" burst out Branwen, surprising everyone. "It's you two! Yes, Swickwit is a little chaotic, but it's not constantly having disasters. Haven't you ever noticed how everything's normal whenever one of you is gone? Then as soon as you're back together, *bam!* It's all commotion and curses and battles again. It's extremely disruptive."

There were several *oohs* at this. Dorian and Beryl nodded.

Ava looked to Tinabella. "She might be right," she said. "That could explain why the entanglement went so wrong. Maybe you and I really shouldn't try to combine our magic."

"You're like two summer thunderheads meeting over a cornfield," said Opal.

"Or two rhino chickens in the same pen," Wolfgang said.

"Or two total show-offs who always have to be the center of attention," said Dorian, his expression mulish.

Jonsi raised a hand a few benches over.

"Why didn't you tell any of us about your plans?" he asked.

"Yeah," said Jadis. "Did you not trust us, or what?"

Ava glanced at Tinabella. "I think that's maybe part of it," she said. "We thought you might tell Gern or whoever. But also Vivienne feels like *our* problem. You know? We've both made her stronger by accident—"

"Partly by accident," Tinabella cut in.

"Partly by accident," continued Ava. "And that makes it our fault she keeps attacking the school."

"That's exactly what we've been saying!" said Branwen.

"So you were trying to clean up your own mess?" asked Carmelie.

Ava nodded. "Totally."

"Plus we also wanted the glory," said Tinabella, who had apparently decided to go for total honesty. "'Cause can you imagine if we actually did it? If you woke up in the morning and the storm was gone and the teachers were back, and it was all down to me and Ava?"

The class considered.

"That would be pretty cool, I guess," Wolfgang said. "You know all the older kids would be talking about it."

"They'd be super jealous," said Beryl.

Ava watched the spark of temptation spread around the room. Some of their classmates might be shocked by what she and Tinabella had done, but everyone here was officially wicked, according to the world outside, and all of them could hear the call of glory.

"How are we feeling about Ava and Tinabella's explanation?" Crow asked.

Ava's stomach flip-flopped again as her classmates looked at one another, raising eyebrows and shrugging.

"I'm over it, I guess," said Opal. "But I think they should apologize."

The rest of the class agreed, and Ava and Tinabella both managed awkward but sincere apologies.

"Cool," said Crow. He smiled at Ava. "Feel better?"

"Yes, actually," Ava said, smiling back.

"You still look kind of angry, though, Tinabella," noted Henry.

Tinabella grunted through her scowl. "I'm angry it didn't work. I spent weeks reading books and making plans, and I'm really, *really* good at both of those things. It should have been a breeze."

"Did you learn anything useful, at least?" asked Crow.

Ava nodded. "We learned that wickedness won't win against the storm. Everything we threw at it made it worse."

"What exactly did you try?"

Between them, Ava and Tinabella detailed the ten poisons, the countless curses, and their complicated attempt at entanglement.

"Whoa," said Crow.

"Okay, I'm impressed now," Dorian said.

"So that's where those bottles from my laboratory went," said Jadis.

"Why wickedness, though?" Margo asked Tinabella. "I mean, why spend all your time in detention just on that?"

Tinabella sat up. "Seriously? Because it worked for Vivienne! It's still working for Vivienne!" Her eyes smoldered. "I was born into a super-rich, totally powerful family, which meant I was supposed to be glamorous and popular and inherit all this money and be happy. It's what I dreamed about when I was a kid. And it all got taken away from me when they sent me here. Vivienne must have lost everything when she came here, too, but then she went and got herself the *most* glamour and wealth and power, way more than even my family has, and she used wicked magic to do it. So why shouldn't *I*?" Tinabella glared around at her classmates. "Do any of you get that?"

"Oh sure," said Branwen, shrugging. "I was supposed to be a candlemaker, and I want to be rich and glamorous and stuff, too."

"Same," said Ava. "And I was supposed to be a brick moss farmer."

"I was supposed to be a stone mason," Matthew said.

"Seriously?" Dorian turned to him. "My mom and dad wanted me to go into geology."

Just like that they were going around the room, each

Nettle student revealing the life their family had expected for them before their early magic and supposed wickedness swept it all away.

For Opal it was train conductor. For Beryl, carpentry. Everyone in Jonsi's family went into dentistry, while Wolfgang's parents were convinced their son was going to become the best actor in Oz. Carmelie was supposed to take over her aunt's flower business one day. Henry, turning pink and shooting a quick glance at Ava, mumbled about his parents wanting him to follow in their footsteps in local government. Jadis was supposed to be a beekeeper. Margo a cheesemonger. Crow didn't know what his family would have wanted, but shared that when he was little, he'd always dreamed of being an animal doctor.

"Why didn't I know any of this?" Carmelie asked after everyone had shared.

"Seriously!" said Ava.

"Who even are all you people?" Branwen laughed.

Beryl stabbed a hand in the air. "This is super awesome," she said. "But what are we doing about, you know, everything? The Midwinter tests are the day after tomorrow."

"Oh! That reminds me," Matthew jumped in. "How does the testing work, Crow? Like, physically."

Ava sat up. She hadn't considered that part.

"All I know is we go into the clock," answered Crow, nodding at the glowing timepiece. "I can't tell you more than that,

’cause I guess you only get to remember what happens in there if you pass.”

“You’ll remember this year, then!” said Margo. “Woo, Crow!”

Crow smiled. “We’ll see. Beryl is right, though—we need to decide what we’re doing these next couple days. We’re almost caught up on the blackboard lists, so we could just keep reviewing for the test. Or . . .”

He paused, his cheeks going a little pink.

“Or what?” demanded Carmelie.

“Or maybe we take on the storm as a group?”

There was a pause, then absolutely everyone was talking at once.

Ava realized her jaw was hanging open.

“I mean, it makes sense, right?” Crow hollered over the uproar. “The storm is super distracting! I bet we’ll all test way better if it’s gone. And if we can’t beat it, at least we’ll know we tried.”

“Are you just trying to make yourself look extra good once Warden Pike gets back?” called Wolfgang.

Crow blushed even pinker.

“He is!” squealed Beryl. “Everybody! Crow’s getting ambitious!”

There was a fierce new energy in the Round Room, one Ava had never sensed there before.

“Let’s do it!”

"Yeah!"

"That storm won't know what hit it!"

"Vivienne Morderay better watch out!"

Ava felt like she and Tinabella had been sharing significant looks all morning, but there was no way to avoid another one now.

Carmelie saw them.

"Oh, don't look like that, you two," she said.

"But they're cheering Crow for suggesting exactly what we just had to apologize for," said Tinabella. Ava nodded.

Carmelie pressed a dramatic hand to her forehead. "Oh my Oz, you two are so stuck in your own world. Didn't you notice he asked *all of us*? That's the difference. He respected us enough to invite us to try. So we're respecting him back."

"Oh," said Tinabella.

"Got it," said Ava. "Thanks."

Crow held up his hands again. "Now, wait, we have to be certain," he called. "Does anybody who still has their name on the blackboard want us to focus on Midwinter testing instead?"

The "No!" that followed filled the Round Room to overflowing.

"Then, okay." Crow's bright smile matched the eager excitement zinging around the room. "We've got less than two days to figure out how to defeat the unbeatable storm and save our school. Let's start planning some serious magic!"

29

OPPOSITE DAY

The students of Nettle spent the rest of their first *sort out how to stop an unstoppable storm* morning hard at work in the classroom.

The one concrete clue they had was that everything that had been tried so far had failed. Crow made a list on the back of the blackboard:

The Teachers	*Unknown advanced magic (net? web?)*
Broom Students	*Unknown advanced magic (hook? claw?)*
Ava & Tinabella	*Wicked magic (poison, curses, entanglement)*
Gern	*Gargoyle magic (spear and shield?)*

"Well, cool," said Margo, "at least we know what not to do."

"What's left, though?" asked Wolfgang. "It's not like we can mathcantation the storm away."

Everybody started talking at once. Tinabella clapped her hands.

"Okay, ugh, I am so gonna regret this," she announced. "But I had an idea based on . . . well . . ."

She looked over at Crow, who wrinkled his forehead, then gasped.

"Soup?" he yelled. "Is it soup?! Please please please let it be soup!"

Tinabella sighed. "It's soup." She waited for Crow to stop squealing. "There's this thing in South Oz called Opposite Soup. The recipe is basically impossible to write down, because the only rule is that every ingredient has to be the opposite of what you actually have."

"I remember that soup!" cried Opal. "The old lady across the alley always used to make it."

"I'm from South Oz and I've never heard of it," declared Dorian.

"I have," said Carmelie. "It's a total delicacy. We had it at the Fancy Hat Festival once. But what does this have to do with the storm?"

Tinabella nodded at Crow's list. "Simple. Since we know everything up there definitely doesn't work, we figure out how to do the opposite."

An enthusiastic debate followed while everyone tried to sort out what the opposite of the items on their list might be.

Eventually, it was decided that the opposite of a net was a bowl and the opposite of a hook was a fan, although since no one had a clue exactly what magic the teachers and Broom students had used in the first place, the point was kind of moot.

"I mean," said Tinabella, "we'd look pretty silly standing on the roof waving a bowl and fan at the storm."

Nobody knew how to figure out the opposite of Gern's spear and shield, either. Gargoyle magic was nothing like human magic, and Jonsi noted that a spear and shield were already opposites of each other. They all agreed this was true but confusing, and Matthew made the whole situation worse by asking what the opposite of a gargoyle was.

Crow sidled over to Ava, Tinabella, and Henry at that point to whisper, "This is just like the impossible questions the needle lady asked us under the school! Remember? *What's the opposite of a buffalo?*"

"Ugh, that was so annoying," said Tinabella.

"I bet there isn't even an answer to that one," Ava said.

"Seriously?" interrupted Jadis, who was sitting nearby and apparently eavesdropping. "The opposite of a buffalo is a peppermint candy. I thought everyone knew that."

"Oh," Henry said as the friends all blinked. "That's, um, good to know."

With all other options off the table, the class decided to work on doing the opposite of everything Ava and Tinabella had done.

A decisive vote determined that the opposite of poison was croutons, the opposite of curses were blessings, and the opposite of entanglement was being left alone with a good book.

The Nettle students all felt very good about these decisions, until Opal pointed out that they were unlikely to disrupt the storm with croutons, and leaving it alone was the actual opposite of what they were trying to do in the first place.

That left blessings.

"Are we seriously talking about taking on Vivienne Morderay with *blessings*?" Dorian said. "This is Swickwit. No one here knows any."

"We're not taking on Vivienne directly," Ava reminded him. "We're breaking her hold on the storm through arcane resonance."

"Will you explain that again?" Margo asked.

Tinabella explained.

"I guess enough blessings could maybe do the trick," mused Carmelie. "Only, Dorian's right: Does anybody know even one?"

Nobody did, but Crow had a solution.

"We'll check out every book on blessings the library has once the portal doors are open," he said. "I guess until then we should just keep studying?"

"Wait!" Branwen shouted. "I have another idea! You know how we all have, like, our original wicked magic? The one that got us sent here?"

"Yeah . . ." said Crow.

"Well, what if we all learn how to do the opposite of that?"

Eyebrows went up around the classroom.

"Think about it," Branwen went on. "That magic was where we all started, right? Professor Mulch taught us how to use it as a doorway to everything else. So it should be easy to go back and just, like, do it differently. You know, now that we're better at magic and everything. Just do what we did before, but completely not the same. The un-wicked version."

"That got less convincing the more you talked," said Jadis.

"She's got a point, though," said Carmelie.

"It's better than studying," Matthew said. "It might even help us on the tests!"

Soon Crow was clearing off the back of the blackboard to start a new list of everyone's original magic skill.

Jonsi	*Makes the sound of unbearable loneliness.*
Margo	*Paralyzes people in place when she sings.*
Carmelie	*Conjures hypnotic candy/pastry houses.*
Branwen	*Gathers and controls scary shadows.*
Jadis	*Freezes stone so cold it shatters.*
Wolfgang	*Creates stinging sparks by holding his breath.*
Dorian	*Swaps around people's faces.*
Matthew	*Can see the worst memory of your life when touching you.*
Beryl	*Summons army of evil ceramic dolls by rubbing knuckles together.*

Opal	*Wiggles ears to make fingernails grow super long/wrap around things.*
Ava	*Water magic.*
Tinabella	*Invisible while running.*
Henry	*Duck and return.*

Crow stood back, eyeing the list.

"Some of these look pretty clear, opposite-wise," he said. "But I dunno, Ava? Henry? Tinabella? Your powers weren't all that wicked to begin with."

"I know, thank you," said Ava.

"How dare you?" said Tinabella.

"Wait," Opal said. "Crow, what about your power?"

Margo sat up. "Ooh, yeah! We still don't know his first magic."

"Didn't he say it was dangerous once?" Jadis asked Jonsi.

"Well, I wasn't planning on—" Crow began, but the class was having none of it.

"Tell us!" shouted Beryl.

"Yeah, tell us!"

"Tell us! Tell us!"

The chant spread, leaving Crow standing there twisting the chalk in his hands, his bottom lip clamped between his teeth. Ava watched him with a pang, wishing she could think of some way to rescue him, but it was his secret in the end, and telling had to be his decision.

At last something seemed to give in Crow's face, and he spun to the blackboard, scribbling quickly along the bottom.

The chanting stopped as he stood back, letting everyone see what he'd written:

Crow Bone Fire.

"No. Way," said Carmelie into the sudden silence.

"Please don't judge me." Crow sounded close to tears. "It's just something I can do. Please don't start thinking of me as Bone Fire Guy."

"What's Bone Fire?" whispered Opal.

Mouths around the room fell open as Carmelie explained.

"And you can actually control it?" Wolfgang asked Crow. "You can use this Bone Fire thing on purpose, whenever you want?"

Crow nodded, hanging his head. "Yeah."

"Whoa."

There was another full, heavy silence, then:

"That's so cool!"

"You must be the wickedest kid here!"

"I can't even picture that much power!"

"I am beyond jealous."

"Will you show us? Right now?"

"I wish I could be like Crow."

"I can't believe he kept that secret!"

Every kid in Nettle was impressed by Crow's admission. None of them shrank away.

Ava's heart went all mushy again at the happy relief on Crow's face. She remembered how reluctantly he had shared his secret with her and Henry during their escape, his fear of being seen as evil just because he had this skill, of people never looking past this one little part of him.

Now here he was, the leader of the class, and thanks to Bone Fire, more liked and respected than ever.

"Okay, okay," Crow said, quieting the room. "You're all super nice. And no, I won't be demonstrating Bone Fire." There was a loud *aww.* "But Branwen's idea was a really good one, so let's get started. We've definitely got plenty to do."

With no opposite-able core magic to work from, Ava, Tinabella, and Henry spent the morning watching their classmates figure out theirs. Dorian grumbled that it wasn't fair none of them would be contributing, but when Tinabella pointed out that the opposite of her magic was literally standing still and being visible, he let the issue drop.

Crow didn't attempt to oppositize his power, either, because of the safety risk. Everyone accepted this, though Matthew did try to figure out the opposite of Bone Fire for fun. His final suggestion of *Skin Water* seemed like a winner at first, until Margo said that was just sweat, so Crow kept busy wandering the classroom giving out high fives and encouragement.

The class worked hard the rest of the morning, and everyone was ready for a break when lunchtime rolled around.

"What's everybody looking forward to most?" Branwen asked when they were settled down with moss jelly sandwiches and spiced apple pie. "After the storm's gone, I mean, and we're heroes, and we've all passed Midwinter testing."

"I just want to get back to clubs," Carmelie said. "It's been weeks since I baked a batch of salted caramel buttercrunch cookies."

Opal nodded. "Same, but with juggle club. I was just getting good at that Merlin's Zoomies pattern."

Everyone looked to Jonsi and Henry.

"Oh!" Henry looked flustered. "I didn't think anybody really noticed Poetry Club."

"You're part of the class, aren't you?" said Beryl. "Of course we notice you."

"We're excited as well," Jonsi reported, gazing at his shoes. "I've been working on a new way to express emotional pain through limericks. Like this." He cleared his throat. "There once was a witch from Mount Marmalade—"

"Amazing!" interrupted Carmelie. "Thanks, Jonsi."

After lunch the portal doors reopened, and it was decided Ava and the others should make themselves useful researching blessings while the rest of the class kept working on their core magic.

"I hope the older kids aren't still in here," Ava said to Crow,

Henry, and Tinabella as she closed the library door behind them. "I'm tired of this place being so crowded all the time."

"Um, I think you got your wish," said Henry.

Ava and the others stopped, staring.

The library was completely deserted.

"Good thing *this* isn't creepy," said Tinabella, stalking forward to peer down the aisles.

"Where do you think they are?" asked Henry.

Ava shook her head. "They better not be out planning something super reckless and dangerous."

"Like us?" Crow said with a grin.

"It's the calm before the storm," declared Tinabella. "Now, forget about them and come on! We don't have much time!"

Even using Tinabella's keyword spell, the four of them had a surprisingly tricky task finding books that could teach them blessings. Most of the books the spell sent them to were fairy tales, full of godmothers and spinning wheels and heavy sleepers. They all got excited when Henry emerged from the stacks with a book called *Blessings of the Frond,* but it turned out to be a deeply boring guide to folding palm leaves into interesting shapes.

"Do you think we could make our own blessings?" Ava asked an increasingly grumpy Tinabella. "Like, try to do reverse versions of the curses we did before?"

"Reverse curse versions!" said Crow. "That's fun to say. You should write that down for a poem, Henry."

"Focus!" Tinabella snapped. "And yeah. If we don't find better stuff soon, we might have to go with homemade and hope for the best."

They kept searching into the evening, finally heading off to dinner with a disappointing seven books, none of them all that useful.

"I hope Burdock comes through," said Tinabella. She'd left the librarian a note asking for help with their search, blaming the urgency on their upcoming Midwinter testing. "Or all we're gonna do tomorrow is make Vivienne Morderay laugh."

Ava was relieved at first to see the older students at dinner that night, filling the hall with their gray and copper robes. Then she noticed how subdued they were, talking softly in groups, focused and serious.

Something was definitely up.

She just hoped it wouldn't interfere with the Nettles' plans.

Back in Nettle Tower, the rest of the class proudly showed the blackboard list to Crow. Every single one of them, it turned out, had succeeded in learning an opposite version of their core wicked magic.

Jonsi	Makes the sound of unbearable loneliness. *Makes the sound of comfortable contentment.*
Margo	Paralyzes people in place when she sings. *Makes people happy-dance when she sings.*

Carmelie	Conjures hypnotic candy/pastry houses. *Basically the same but not hypnotic.*
Branwen	Gathers and controls scary shadows. *Basically the same but using them for good.*
Jadis	Freezes stone so cold it shatters. *Creates a nice, relaxing warmth.*
Wolfgang	Creates stinging sparks by holding his breath. *Creates tickling puff balls.*
Dorian	Swaps around people's faces. *Gives people super-realistic face painting if they want.*
Matthew	Can see the worst memory of your life when touching you. *Sees people's happiest memory and lets them see it, too.*
Beryl	Summons army of evil ceramic dolls by rubbing knuckles together. *Summons tiny friendly stuffed animals.*
Opal	Wiggles ears to make fingernails grow super long/wrap around things. *Makes fingernails extra strong. Also into tools as needed.*

"You all are amazing!" said Crow when he got to the bottom, and everyone looked incredibly proud of themselves.

Of course, there had to be demonstrations. The rest of the

evening passed full of laughter, borderline chaos, and more fizzy, cheerful magic than Nettle Tower had probably seen in centuries.

The whole class was watching Wolfgang and Margo try to merge their new powers in a united dance attack when there was a knock at the library door.

Opal opened it to find Burdock, his six arms supporting a towering stack of books.

"Oh, thank Oz!" yelled Tinabella, rushing over with Ava, who thanked Burdock again and again.

"Goodness, it's no troubling," rumbled the giant beetle-man, passing over the tomes. "I'm just gratitude to see you all workening so hard, and showing such enthusiasmum for your tests even without your teachers here to guide you." He paused, tilting his head. "I don't recall the tests coverating blessings, though. Is that new?"

Crow gave an awkward cough, and everyone became very busy looking anywhere but at the librarian.

"It's just in case," Tinabella said. "We want to be super, completely, totally sure we're ready for anything."

"And that, Tinabella," said Burdock, "is why I like you all so muchness. It's a goodly thing you asked for my help, though. These books are kept in the Sunshine section, which is restrictated to staff. I mean, blessings!" He gave a dramatic shiver. "They scare the scales off me!"

It had been an exciting, busy day for everyone, and not

long after Burdock's visit, yawns began replacing the Round Room chatter.

"Hey, no all-nighters, you two!" Crow called to Ava and Tinabella as they headed for their room with their arms full of blessing books. "This time tomorrow we'll be tackling the storm, and it's Midwinter testing the morning after that. We all need plenty of sleep so we're ready!"

Ava smiled, waving good night with her elbow.

Crow was correct, sleep probably was a good idea, but the books were right there, and her mind was still too busy for bed.

In any case she'd already done all the test prep she could handle. And she'd faced Vivienne Morderay more times than anyone else here.

How much more ready could she get?

30

PREPARING FOR BATTLE

Ava and Tinabella did stay up most of the night reading—there was no stopping Tinabella when she had a stack of books in front of her—so they were both yawning as they entered the Round Room for breakfast the next day.

Their late-night studies had been worth it, though. They were decent at casting blessings now, and had done enough practicing to be able to teach the rest of their classmates.

Ava glanced at the countdown clock, smiling at the enormous fuchsia 1 fizzing with gold and rainbow sparks. She thought back again to the morning the storm appeared and Professor Mulch's lecture about the clock: *Think of who you want to be when it says one!*

That felt like months ago. So much had happened since: epic struggles, new magic, and more than one uncomfortable lesson. Overall, Ava thought she was reasonably happy with who she was now that the day was finally here.

"Whoa! What happened to you two?" Henry asked as Ava and Tinabella reached the breakfast table.

Both girls looked at each other. Then they burst out laughing.

They'd been so tired they'd forgotten to reset all the

blessings they'd tried on each other the night before, and Ava's hair sat coiled in a two-foot mountain of fairy-tale ringlets, while Tinabella's silver skin sparkled with iridescent hearts and daisies.

They undid the blessings and loaded up their plates, joining their chattering, excited classmates for what might just be the most important day of their lives.

Ava and Tinabella's basic blessings class started immediately after breakfast.

Most blessings worked by combining magical energy with a short rhyming phrase or poem. Done properly, this created an eyeball-sized glowing bubble, usually pink or green, that could be lobbed at the lucky recipient.

Unlike curses, blessings had to be made in the moment, so there was no storing them up in folded bits of paper this time. Also unlike curses, blessings were never permanent. The whole class was disappointed to learn that all blessings, no matter how powerful, wore off, usually sooner rather than later.

As for what kind of blessings the Nettles would use to disrupt the storm, Burdock's books offered long lists of classics, including wit, poise, a keen sense of humor, and fresh breath.

"Is everyone good with picking five or ten and memorizing them?" Ava asked, passing the books around. "I don't think it matters what we choose, just so long as you can remember and cast them okay later."

The class got right to work. There were some mishaps, of course: Dorian managed to give Wolfgang a scraggly silver beard when he switched words in a good table manners blessing, and Carmelie's first peaceful dreams attempt somehow doused Opal in a shower of glittering sand. But overall things went well.

By midday they all had a handle on basic blessings, and after lunch the Nettles threw themselves into practicing. This quickly morphed into a competitive blessings battle, however, and Crow had to put a stop to things before someone got hurt.

"It's not that I don't want us all to get better," he yelled over the noise of Jonsi, Margo, and Beryl jumping so high they could slap the ceiling. "It's just that we should probably keep our feet on the ground while we can."

Once everyone settled down, Ava and Tinabella took over again to discuss that night's battle plan against the storm.

"The big thing to remember," Ava said, "is that we're not trying to *attack* the storm. Wicked magic just made it stronger, and we think any kind of fighting might do the same thing. What we want is to tip the balance. You know, overwhelm it with so much good magic it makes Vivienne lose her grip."

"Basically, we want to be really annoying and disruptive," clarified Tinabella.

"That'll be easy with you two leading us," Carmelie said with a grin.

Ava turned to Tinabella. "Do you think we should start with everyone doing their un-wicked powers first?" she asked. "Since they've got more oomph?"

Tinabella nodded. "For sure. I think we'll know right away if it's working. If it's not, we can start pouring on the blessings and hope it all piles up."

"Ooh, I cannot wait," said Jadis. "We are gonna bless the swirls off that storm!"

Ava beamed at the excitement in the room. Even with all their goofing around, her classmates were more focused than she'd ever seen them.

"It's kind of wild how much we can learn in two days, isn't it?" Matthew said.

Branwen gave a proud nod. "Seriously! They really should let us teach ourselves more often."

They entered the dining hall as a group that evening, laughing and talking until the kids in front stopped dead, leaving the others to bump into them. Everyone stared.

The dining hall was completely empty.

Candles burned in the chandeliers, and flames crackled in the giant fireplace, but there was not one single other student in sight.

"Well," said Beryl. "Cobweb and Cauldron are definitely up to something."

"It better not be happening tonight," Dorian said.

Beryl sighed. "Bet it is."

Ava, Tinabella, Henry, and Crow had all seen the enormous dining hall empty during the adventure of the Nettle Smith, but the others had not, and there was a general round of whooping, shouting, and running up and down the long rows of tables before they settled down to their meal.

It felt very strange to be sitting together at their usual table with the silent school spreading out around them. The emptiness slowly squeezed the enthusiasm from the group, leaving behind an anxious, uneasy mood. Even Crow found it hard to keep up his cheerful banter as the candles flickered and the clink of their forks and spoons echoed back at them in the cavernous space.

The group's nerves doubled back in Nettle Tower. Everyone milled around, checking and rechecking spellwork, cracking jokes and laughing too much. People kept asking Crow if it was time. Ava began to feel as though they were the last living beings in all of Oz, and the future of the whole world depended on what she and her classmates managed to do that night.

She knew she was probably being dramatic; Warden Pike was still out there somewhere, and would be doing his utmost to rescue them. But she couldn't shake the feeling he should have succeeded by now. It was unsettling to consider it might actually be down to them.

Plenty of her classmates, she discovered, were feeling the same.

"Are we sure about this?" she overheard Matthew asking Carmelie as she passed them in the hall. "I mean, taking on Vivienne Morderay? We're just a bunch of kids."

"Crow says we should try," Carmelie replied. "I trust him."

"But what if it all goes super wrong?"

"Then at least we won't have to worry about the tests tomorrow!"

"Ha! Wait, that's actually not funny, though."

"Look, if it goes wrong, we run back inside. We're totally safe here. We hunker down, take the tests tomorrow morning, and wait for Warden Pike to fix things."

"I guess . . ."

Retreating to her own room for a little peace and quiet, Ava flopped back onto her bed and heaved a sigh. Deep down, she knew if she hadn't run away from school all those months ago, hadn't insisted she knew better than everyone and was in the wrong place, she never would have met Vivienne and given her the final pin from the Lost Collar of Arboc. That meant Vivienne would never have come looking for the instruction manual, and Tinabella would never have tried to betray them all to become her apprentice, and . . . well, none of these dangerous disasters would have happened. Yes, Vivienne was the one doing the attacks, but in the end Ava was the one who'd made them possible.

She swallowed a sour twist of guilt. She'd always thought she was making the right choices at the time, good choices, necessary choices. But looking back over the chain of events she'd started, now she knew exactly where they led, it was hard not to feel undeniably wicked.

Although, she considered as her thoughts spun, she knew what true wickedness felt like now, and guilt had definitely not been part of it. So maybe the heaviness filling her chest was actually a good sign, after all.

A burst of excited clamor echoed in from the hallway, and Ava let herself quirk a smile at the ceiling. There was one definite silver lining to all this trouble: Her class had never been closer. In all their weird and awkward combinations, the residents of Nettle Tower had become true friends these last few weeks, and that was a real blessing.

One she hoped would last.

Finally, as the glow of the storm grew brighter amid the oncoming night, Crow gave the word, and fourteen brave kids gathered in the classroom to undertake their mission. They stood close together, shuffling their feet and shooting one another nervous smiles. Branwen made a dash back to her room for an extra scarf, and Wolfgang stalled for three whole minutes looking for his lucky raven beak, which turned out to have been in his pocket the whole time.

"Remember," Crow told them when they were finally ready, his voice just the tiniest bit shaky, "we're not fighting the storm, we're being positively disruptive. Un-wicked magic first, then if that doesn't work, we start casting blessings. Got it?"

Everyone nodded.

Crow turned to the missing window, his face set.

"Then let's go."

31

VIVIENNE

Vivienne Morderay examined the objects covering the amber worktop in the east wing of her lair and began to seriously wonder if she was okay.

For two days now she'd been biding her time waiting for her potential apprentices in Swickwit to send their next message. She should have been rampaging triumphantly across Oz, of course, but she couldn't leave now, not when those girls were trying so hard to impress her and win her favor. It wouldn't be fair on them.

So she'd hung around instead, wandering her lair, throwing the occasional cricket to her new pet birds and racking her brains for things to do. Somehow, she had settled on knitting.

Knitting.

Vivienne picked through the pile on the worktop, considering the possibility that she might have been cursed. Where else would the idea have come from? And the memory of how to do it? She hadn't even thought about knitting since she was small, when her mother and the other carnival ladies sat around clacking their needles and drinking very strong beverages in the evenings after shows. She had been forced to learn how back then, since everyone thought she would grow up to be just another nobody like them.

Of course, everyone had always been wrong about Vivienne Morderay.

But why had her knitting memories—the sound, the steady shaping, the warmth of her mother's colorful scarves—arisen now, after almost a century?

It wasn't as though Vivienne would ever wear a knitted garment. Certainly not *these*. She pinched a blue creation between her fingertips and held it up, letting the folds flollop onto the table. What *was* it? Matching elephant ear-warmers? A sweater for a gargly-goyle? An upside-down map of Oz?

She shuddered, returning the vile thing to the pile as a sudden surge of feelings rocked her, flashes of childhood memories crashing against a jittery sort of panic about her future plans. Something tender pulsed just below her ribs as she reached out to a lumpy yellow sock, squeezing its scratchy softness between her fingers . . .

Why did she feel so lost?

Anger abruptly ignited within her, and with one clawing gesture and a shouted word, Vivienne burned every last thing on the worktop to ash.

Blood pumped in her ears as she got to her feet, pacing the otak-skin rugs, the stench of burned wool wafting in her wake. She needed whatever this was to end. She needed to feel like her magnificent, triumphant self again!

Vivienne fed the anger until it seared away her confusion and the feelings that had caused it, replacing it all with a stern, steely concentration.

She strode to her largest window, looking south over the country that would soon be hers. The tail end of sunset filled the western sky, towering peach and bruised rose, beautiful against the wash of deepest blue coming from the east.

Somewhere out there two young girls were battling for her attention, hoping to earn a place by her side.

Vivienne ignored the leap her heart tried to give at the thought of having an apprentice, of regular companionship, of someone always there to lecture and order around and talk to.

The girls had taken too much of her time already and caused too many complications.

She would give them tonight to truly impress her. Just one more night.

Then her conquest of Oz would begin.

32
THE BATTLE

The roots went out of their way to be helpful as the Nettle students climbed out their classroom window and made their way up to the roof.

They all gathered around the spike, gawking just as they had on their very first visit the morning the storm arrived. Their mood could not have been more different, though. Neither could the storm. That first whirlwind of air and spells and glass seemed downright quaint compared to the glowing, flaming, smoking, howling chaos surging above them in the night.

"Wow," Jonsi said, coming to stand beside Ava with his head thrown back. "All of that was you and Tinabella?"

Ava looked up, remembering Jonsi could see her and Tinabella's magic swirling through the storm.

"Yep," she said as an eye-watering patch of poison colors swept by.

"Scary," said Jonsi.

Ava agreed. Thinking about everything she'd done in her own personal Wicked Mode made her head spin. She was more grateful than she could say to be back to her regular self.

The Nettle students were standing close together again,

and Ava caught Branwen's eye, then Henry's, sharing the same nervous agreement: Now that they were up here, their plan was actually quite terrifying.

"So what happens next?" Carmelie asked, nudging Crow. "I know we're doing our un-wicked magic, but do we just, like, start?"

Crow nodded, his eyes extra wide in the fiery green light. Ava felt for him. He was good at being in charge, and it had been his idea for the whole class to take on the storm. But she didn't think Crow realized until right that second the sheer danger of what they were all about to do.

"I guess," he said. "Let's, uh, let's have everybody line up. Maybe right here?"

Soon, the un-wicked magic squad was lined up in two rows across the roof. Crow went back and forth making sure each of them had plenty of room and wasn't too near the edge, then joined Ava, Henry, and Tinabella at the spike.

"Okay," he called. "When I say *one,* everybody tap into your powers. On *two,* get your magic ready. On *three,* um, you know . . . go."

Ava bit her lip. It wasn't the most inspirational speech she'd ever heard.

"One!" yelled Crow.

Most of the students stood up straighter as they called on their power. Carmelie brought her hands together in front of her.

"Two!"

The tension on the roof increased.

"Three!" Crow shouted. "Go!"

Nothing happened.

Heads turned as the un-wicked squad eyed one another, all of them waiting for someone else to go first.

Then Margo began to sing, her voice filling the air with an irresistibly joyful melody, and the dam broke.

Jonsi's hum of perfect contentment joined Margo's song. Waves of relaxing warmth from Jadis amplified the aroma of the gingerbread houses Carmelie began conjuring one after another. Beryl summoned armies of adorable stuffed animals from the stone roof while Wolfgang sent tickling puff balls spilling across it beside her. Branwen took charge of distribution, gathering shadows from around the school to scoop up the pastry houses, puff balls, and stuffed animals and fling them into the storm, where they flashed in vivid colors before being swept away.

It was harder to see Opal's, Matthew's, and Dorian's powers in action, since as far as anyone knew the storm didn't have memories, fingernails, or a face. But all three of them were staring hard into the clouds, muttering, and Ava spotted wild new patterns appearing on the storm's surface.

"Is it working?" Henry asked, shifting from foot to foot.

"Something's happening!" said Crow. "Look!"

Ava did, and saw their new colors and patterns were joining together, swirling across the wind to form a band of berry purple, sky blue, and buttery yellow.

"Yes!" Ava shouted. "I think it's happening!"

But even as she said it, the colorful band shattered into a thousand pieces, and a sound came from the thunderclouds roiling in the center of the storm, a sound that sent Ava right back to the moment she'd first heard it under a certain circus tent: a deep, cruel, echoing laughter.

The un-wicked squad broke off, scrambling back to huddle around Crow as the clouds above surged and joined, forming themselves into the towering head, shoulders, and feathery mane of Vivienne Morderay.

Everyone who hadn't screamed yet did so.

"Well," boomed Vivienne, her smoke-gray face peering down at Nettle Tower. "Hello tooo youuu, toooo!"

Glancing around, Ava discovered she was now out in front of the class, Tinabella beside her.

"I see youuu have brought friends, girls!" Vivienne said, her cloud eyes roving over them. "How delightful! But I cannot take them all as apprentices, youuu know."

Ava's insides were churning worse than the boiling lake. How had things gone so wrong?

Vivienne turned her gaze to the shattered remains of their un-wicked attempt, the ice-cream colors disintegrating into the storm.

"An odd way tooo get my attention," she said. "What exactly were youuu trying—"

A ripping sound cut her off, an echoing slash like a thousand pieces of paper being torn in two, and the Nettles goggled as clusters of Cauldron and Cobweb kids began appearing on every other tower across Swickwit.

"Oh no," groaned Tinabella. "They're trying something."

It looked like she was right. One student per tower held up a staff of golden metal, and a great shout went up, a spell Ava could not follow. The next moment, a golden spiderweb of light sprang into being, arcing from tower top to tower top.

It seemed to be a serious upgrade to the spell web the Broom students had tried, and Ava's heart leapt as, with another shout, the golden tangle went soaring into the sky directly at the Vivienne cloud.

Will it work? she wondered, biting her lip. *Will the older kids save the day after all?*

The web found its target, the golden threads crisscrossing Vivienne's face, splitting and expanding and squeezing . . .

Vivienne's growl was pure thunder.

"If there is one thing I hate," she bellowed, "it is being interrupted!"

With a shake of her head, the threads shattered. Giant hands appeared out of the clouds, and before the older students could do more than shout in alarm, Vivienne had cracked every golden staff with a snap of her fingers and sent the remains of the spiderweb hurtling back where they came from.

Less than a minute after making their grand appearance, each one of the Cobweb and Cauldron students was trapped in place under a sticky magical net.

Cries of dismay competed with the noise of the storm, but Vivienne raised a finger, and every last voice was abruptly cut off.

Ava and Tinabella shared a panicked look. They were really, truly, completely on their own now.

Ava had a sudden wild urge to lead a retreat back inside Nettle Tower. Would they even make it, though? And what would be the point if they did? Vivienne would still be here. They couldn't back down until they'd tried absolutely everything, and Ava and her classmates still had one trick up their sleeves.

"As I was *saying*," Vivienne purred, with a significant look at the trapped students. "I have mostly enjoyed your attempts tooo win my attention, girls. Though this last one was odd. Goody-goody magic?" She gave an affected shudder. "What were youuu thinking? Still, there is time enough to teach youuu style. Youuu have taste and intelligence, clearly, since youuu are so charmingly dedicated tooo securing a position as my apprentice."

"Um," Carmelie murmured behind Ava, "what's she talking about?"

"Yeah," chimed in Dorian. "What does she mean, *apprentice*?"

Whispers spread among the Nettle students. Ava looked back and saw hurt and suspicion on their faces. Even Crow looked shaken.

She had to set the record straight.

Feeling dangerously exposed, Ava stepped forward.

"Hi!" she yelled up at Vivienne, then immediately felt weird about it. How were you supposed to address the gargantuan floating head of the wicked witch who had captured your school? "Um, hello!" she tried again. "So, we're confused, because we haven't been trying to impress you."

"What?" boomed Vivienne.

Tinabella appeared at Ava's side. "She means stop saying we want to be your apprentices!" she shouted. "I did once, but I don't anymore! And Ava never did!"

Ava flushed, grateful to have Tinabella defending her so publicly, but also feeling distinctly guilty considering it wasn't quite the truth.

Vivienne narrowed her eyes.

"Then why have youuu been showing off?" she called. "Why try tooo impress me over and over with these wicked improoovements tooo my storm?"

"They weren't improvements!" Ava's throat was starting to hurt from all this shouting. "We were trying to take it away from you. Or break your hold, at least."

"Using arcane resonance!" Tinabella added. "You interpreted everything we were doing totally wrong!"

The whispers had become murmurs behind the two girls now, but Ava didn't dare look round.

Vivienne's face scrunched.

"Well, the joke is on youuu," she spat. "Because youuu failed!"

Even in cloud form, Ava knew Vivienne well enough to recognize disappointment in her expression, along with a good dose of embarrassment.

"Not that it would have worked, anyway," Vivienne continued. "Youuu were misguided from the start. *I* am not powering the storm, the Collar of Arboc is, and it cannot be distracted or destroyed."

Vivienne touched one stormy hand to her throat, where a familiar snake-shaped necklace clung, flickers of lightning filling in for the powerful rainbow gems.

Ava drew in a breath of realization, suddenly understanding her vision of gleaming gold and intoxicating power when she'd followed the storm's resonance back to its source.

"Youuu have disappointed me, children!" yelled Vivienne. "Youuu are disappointing, and dull, and boring, and fooolish!"

A swoop of satisfaction swept over Ava. They might not be stopping the storm, but they had succeeded in upsetting Vivienne, and that was better than nothing. They had finally gotten under her skin.

"Oh, don't be like that," Ava called, fighting back a reckless laugh. "You said I had a gift for wickedness before, remember?"

"Yeah," Tinabella added. "And what happened to us having *intelligence and taste* like two minutes ago? Or were you wrong about that, too?"

"Shut up!" boomed Vivienne. "I was not wrong—I was lying! All your magic was uuuseless. Poisons and curses? Ha! Little kid games! Youuu couldn't even dooo entanglement properly!" She paused, and a grin spread across her features, lightning crackling around the edges. "Here, allow me tooo demonstrate."

Vivienne stabbed a finger down toward Nettle Tower, and before any of the Nettle students could do more than flinch, Ava was suddenly ripped from the roof and flying straight up into the air, her school and friends falling away around her, her mind no longer her own.

33

ONLY YOU

If she'd had time to think about it, Ava would have savored her journey soaring through the sky above Swickwit. She was actually flying, zooming up and up over the school and the lake until she was face-to-face with the cloud version of Vivienne.

She didn't have time, though, because Vivienne Morderay's magic was controlling her body and filling her mind.

Ava finally understood what it meant to be entangled. She felt squeezed inside herself, shoved back against her spine. She couldn't move. She couldn't speak. She couldn't focus on anything but Vivienne. And she couldn't feel her own magic.

She could sense the empty air beneath her and hear the roaring storm. She could see the swirling glow all around and the thundercloud shaped like Vivienne. But somehow, she could also see the real Vivienne, standing in a lush, beautiful room full of soft carpets and mysterious artifacts and a golden cage with two strange birds.

Vivienne smiled, giving a flick of one ringed hand, and Ava became aware that she could speak.

She groaned instead.

"Yes, entanglement does take some getting uuused tooo,"

crooned Vivienne. "Your ruuude friend *will* be jealous, won't she? Once again, I have chosen youuu over her. Be proud, little witch. I have seen throuuugh your fooolish failings. I can see the uuuseful apprentice youuu will make for me."

Ava was scared, very scared. She was floating in midair between a storm and a nasty fall onto the towers of her school, and the most powerful wicked witch in all of Oz was inside her head.

But she was also just about fed up.

"Why don't you ever listen?" she said, her voice only shaking a little bit. "I don't want to be your apprentice! I won't! And neither will Tinabella. Even though she'd be incredible at it!" she added. "You'd be super lucky to have her."

Vivienne's beautiful eyes narrowed. "Why speak up for the girl? She is holding youuu back. Anyone can see youuu have nothing in common." She gave a dramatic sigh. "Someday, youuu will learn as I did that no one else can ever truuuly understand youuu."

Her words sparked a memory in Ava, and she found herself quoting the Swickwit motto, "'Only you can know where you have been.'"

Vivienne leaned back, examining her with an odd, searching look. "Exactly," she said, her voice softer than before. "That is one thing this schoool got right."

Ava swallowed. She was alone in a terrible situation, but something she'd said appeared to have struck a nerve with

Vivienne. If words were the only tool she had to work with, she was going to keep talking.

"It is a pretty good motto," she said. "But I, um, don't know if you really understand it." Vivienne bristled, and Ava hurried on, ideas connecting in her mind along with memories of her classmates revealing the lives they were supposed to have lived—actor, train conductor, candlemaker, farmer. "I think it's telling us to remember that that's true for everyone, that we're all the main character to ourselves. And if you do remember that, then other people make more sense. You actually *can* kind of understand them, and if you share your story, too, then they can understand you back." Ava was almost babbling, but her heart was telling her to keep going. "Have you ever shared, Vivienne?" she asked wildly. "Does anyone really know your story?"

For the first time, Ava looked fully into Vivienne Morderay's eyes.

It was like arcane resonance all over again. Ava found herself falling forward as though through a long tunnel, bright, vivid images and flickering bursts of power rushing by until she came to a sudden halt and a scene spread out before her.

She was looking down over the tents and caravans of a circus—or, no, a carnival. It was nothing like the lavish, blood-red big top where she'd first met Vivienne. This was a rundown show, with patchwork tents, drooping banners, and plenty of mud. A soggy sunset hung in the sky overhead, and a girl of no more than seven was crouched outside a cotton candy booth, drawing on the ground with a stick. She had delicate lavender skin and large, unhappy eyes. Ava peered closer and saw she was drawing the outline of a unicorn. As though she could feel someone watching, the girl suddenly looked up, her eyes meeting Ava's.

Another flash, another rush through the flickering tunnel, and Ava was in a dorm room she knew very, very well, the last room on the left at the top of Nettle Tower. The same lavender-skinned girl was sitting on one of the beds, eleven now, or twelve, crying into her hands while loud, laughing voices mocked and shouted at her through the door. It was a miserable scene, especially in the familiar setting, and Ava felt her heart ache. Just like before, the girl seemed to become aware she was being watched and looked up.

The gesture was so precisely the same that for a moment both young Viviennes appeared before Ava, wavering together, and their expressions changed to wide-eyed wonder.

"No!"

Ava felt herself shoved, mind and body, and Vivienne's beautiful grown-up face returned, twisted in fury as it filled her vision.

"Youuu will not mock me!" she growled. "If youuu won't be my apprentice, then youuu won't be a witch, either!"

She raised her hand to the collar, but Ava never found out what spell was coming because suddenly Tinabella was there.

Ava could see her the same way she saw Vivienne, standing on the roof of Nettle Tower but also somehow right beside her. The sense of being squeezed up inside herself grew even more crowded. It was like trying to fit three students into one desk.

"What?!" shrieked Vivienne. "What is—How are youuu doooing this?"

"Neat, huh?" said Tinabella. Ava had never seen her smile so widely before. "It's group magic. I'm leading the whole class like that Broom girl we saw! Check it out!"

Ava felt Tinabella's magic wash over her, and there was the whole line of Nettle classmates stretching back. She drank in the sight of them, feeling a surge of hope as she felt Opal's magic, and Carmelie's, and Dorian's, Jonsi's, Matthew's, Jadis's, Wolfgang's, Branwen's, Henry's, Margo's, Beryl's, and Crow's. Together they formed a heaving hodgepodge of mismatched power, a fierce magical patchwork all channeled through Tinabella's extraordinary self-confidence.

The vision blurred as Vivienne yanked Ava's mind back.

"Answer me, girl!" Vivienne demanded, elbowing Tinabella. "Youuu could not entangle a puddle before. How has your magic advanced so quickly? Your grouuup magic is not enough tooo explain it."

The shock of Tinabella's arrival was wearing off, and Ava, brimming with newfound hope, spoke up. "That's easy," she said. "Tinabella used to be a cookbook."

"What?!"

"It's true," said Tinabella. "*1001 Savory Soups of Oz*. Did you know for East Oz Sunshine Soup you have to puree the skraggle berries until they gelatinize?"

"Don't forget to add the simmering lilies," said Ava, remembering.

"Oh, definitely not!" Tinabella waggled a finger at Vivienne. "The simmering lilies!"

"What is wrong with youuu twooo?" spat Vivienne. "Youuu dare tooo make fun of me?"

Tinabella held up her hands. "Okay, okay, fine. It's mostly because of Jonsi. He's got spell-sight, and he saw what you did when you entangled Ava, then described it to me."

Vivienne relaxed just a touch.

"Ahh, that would make a difference," she said. "And now, what exactly dooo youuu plan tooo dooo? Will youuu fight me for control of your little friend's mind? Youuu know I am stronger. Youuu know youuu will looose."

Ava was surprised at the excitement she felt coming from Tinabella, barely hidden under a careful layer of calm.

"That's probably true," she said. "So I thought I'd fall back on something Ava and I can't seem to help being every time we're together."

Vivienne's lip curled. "And what is that?"

Tinabella smiled. "Disruptive."

Ava didn't see the signal, but she definitely felt the effect as an avalanche of pink and green bubbles began pouring out of Tinabella. She barely had time to register what must have been the whole class's efforts, strengthened through the power of group magic, as Vivienne was hit with blessings for fresh breath, good table manners, wit, clean ears, and so much more.

Bubbles popped and tumbled all around the wicked witch, turning her red teeth white, her feather hair into princess curls, and her eyelashes into tiny butterflies.

All at once Ava regained control of her body. She was still floating in midair high above the school, but she could move her arms and legs again. She could even feel her magic. It was working! Vivienne's hold on her was slipping!

Inspired, she joined in as hard as she could, throwing blessing after blessing at Vivienne, over and over, hurling everything she had at this one final chance—

"ENOUGH!"

Searing white light exploded across Ava's mind. For a moment she lost track of everything: Tinabella, Vivienne, the sensation of floating, her own body.

Then the world returned, along with her companions, only something had changed.

"What did you do?" yelled Tinabella. "Where are the others?"

"What is it?" Ava asked.

"The class is gone! And I'm"—Tinabella turned and twisted—"stuck!"

Vivienne practically purred. She had shaken the blessings off, returning to her usual darkly glamorous self.

"I have severed your little grouuup magic link," she said. "Youuu should have known better than tooo mock me."

Ava opened her mouth, but Vivienne cut her off. "No! Youuu will no longer speak."

Ava tried and found she couldn't. Tinabella's face turned red as she made the same discovery.

Vivienne regarded them. "I must admit, I will miss youuu twooo just the teeniest bit. We have had some . . . interesting discussions. But I cannot allow youuu tooo continuuue interfering with my plans. If neither of youuu will become my apprentice, it is back tooo Plan A: cutting youuu off from magic." She paused, regarding them. "Well? Youuu may try tooo struggle now."

They did.

Ava and Tinabella writhed and fought and thrashed and kicked, they even tried to merge their powers, but nothing had any effect.

Vivienne cackled.

Tinabella fought on, thrashing harder than ever, but Ava, exhausted and overwhelmed, felt herself slipping into despair.

It was like their first entanglement attempt all over again. Nothing she knew how to do could stop what was coming. She could not fight. She couldn't even speak. She and

Tinabella were going to lose their powers, and it was all her fault for thinking she could take on Vivienne and her storm. They were nothing compared to her, just a couple of kids playing with magic, and soon Ava wouldn't even have that anymore. She would never be powerful and important, never return home in triumph, never grow into the one thing in the whole world she knew she wanted to become.

"Say goodbye tooo your spells, little witches!" sang Vivienne, her feathers lifting all around her and her red lacquered teeth gleaming in triumph as she placed seven fingers one by one on the jewels in the Lost Collar of Arboc.

Tinabella turned away. The collar flared, and Ava flinched, instinctively holding up her hands.

The scars on her palms burst into blazing life.

Power rang through Ava as a kaleidoscope of colors erupted between her and Vivienne. The air suddenly smelled of fire and iron. There was a twisting screech of metal.

Vivienne screamed.

The whole world went *MOOWF.*

34

AFTER

Ava fell.

The storm was collapsing.

Ava fell.

Voices were screaming.

Ava fell.

The tower tops zoomed toward her.

Ava fell.

Thwang.

Ava stopped.

For several long moments she simply bounced upside down in the air. Then she felt the tug coiling her from shoulder to ankle.

The roots of Nettle Tower had caught her.

Something strange seemed to be happening to time, and in the seconds it took the roots to carry her back to the tower, Ava saw many things she knew she would never forget.

Gern plummeting out of the fading clouds and dropping with an almighty splash into the lake.

The roiling storm collapsing down on itself, rebuilding the glass hills in a tinkling, splintering rain.

The chain of Broom students falling out of the wind, heading directly for the boiling water.

The lake monster surging out of the darkness, huge teeth bared, catching the students on its shining body so they slid safely to the shore.

The teachers flaring awake one by one, bouncing off the fortress walls in great splashes of magic.

With a thud, Ava landed on the lip of Nettle Tower, only just keeping her footing as the roots retreated. Her classmates rushed her, a blur of faces and voices checking she was okay, but there was still too much happening below to answer. She stared down, distantly aware that Tinabella had an arm around her shoulders as she watched Gern come staggering out of the lake, shaking water from his wings, and the last of the green, glowing, flaming, churning, devouring storm collapsed over the shards of the glass hills, flared once, and died.

For the first time in what felt like years, silence settled over the School for Wicked Witches. Stars twinkled down in a crisp winter sky.

Ava and her classmates stared out, taking in the sight.

And from the side of the lake and every roof and tower top, in complete violation of a thousand years of tradition, all the older students stared back.

35
WARDEN PIKE

Warden Threnody Pike had never seen anything like it in all his long, long, long, long life.

One moment Vivienne Morderay had been blazing with power, her body suspended in midair, her lavish robes billowing around her and phosphorescence shimmering from her black cascade of feathers. Whatever fight she was engaged in, it was clear she was winning.

The next, Vivienne screamed, dropped to the ground, and collapsed in a heap as every speck of light and power in her lair winked out.

Including Warden Pike's magical cage.

Both birds plummeted, and Pike got his wings out just in time, swooping to an awkward but reasonably soft landing on the fur-lined floor. His cagemate wasn't so quick. The other bird landed with a thunk and lay there in the dark, stunned, the sheen of its redecorated feathers just visible in the starlight from the nearest window.

Pike transformed, stretching his shoulders gratefully. His eyes gleamed as he stood statue-still, listening with every one of his senses.

Vivienne Morderay's lair was cold and silent and dead.

Her collection of magical artifacts did not hum. The Radnelac stone in the corner was as dark as any rock on the mountain outside.

Whoever Vivienne had been fighting, they had knocked out her and her entire armory. From a distance. While she was wearing the Lost Collar of Arboc.

How?

Warden Pike was not easily shaken, but his sudden freedom and the shock of what had happened to Vivienne were enough that he almost missed the small sound behind him.

He spun, his counterspell ready only just in time.

The curse Osmuth Rust had thrown ricocheted, shattering a crystal serpent statue. Osmuth jumped back, but Warden Pike was faster, and next moment the man was locked in place, his arms and legs immobile.

Pike conjured a handful of cool blue fire and sent it circling the ceiling.

"Osmuth," he said. "It has been a while."

The trapped figure smiled. He was a handsome man, lean-faced and wiry, with lichen-green skin and a mop of shaggy black hair framing one golden-orange eye and a slashing scar where the other had been. Delicate wave tattoos covered the backs of his hands.

"Good to see you're as quick to judgment as ever, Threnny," said Osmuth Rust.

Warden Pike's jaw pulsed. "I am not the one who tried

to greet an old friend with a bone-splitting curse."

Osmuth huffed. "Oh, that was just a friendly hello. Knew you'd block it. Now how about unfreezing me so we can hug?"

"Why are you here?" asked Warden Pike.

"No hug? Fine. I'm here for the same reason as you: to check on what old Vivienne's up to. Been awfully reclusive since she finished the collar, and that's not like her. Thought maybe she needed a friend. Or some help from an old pal."

It was Warden Pike's turn to huff. "You have been foolish as ever. She has become too powerful. My school is at risk, so I journeyed here to stop her." Pike felt the half-truth heavy on his tongue, but he was not about to admit to Osmuth Rust that he'd been considering asking Vivienne to make a deal.

Osmuth rolled his eyes. "Always with that school! More to Oz than Swickwit, Threnny. Why would Vivienne even spare the old ruin a thought?"

"She has already attacked it."

"You don't say."

"With Dorothy's Gale."

For the first time, Osmuth Rust looked surprised. He whistled. "Well, guess I can see why you'd rush up here and try to stop her, then. Although can't say you did a great job. Getting stuck in a cage? Right away? With me? Ouch. Good thing someone else finished the mission for you."

The two men looked over at Vivienne lying unconscious

on the carpet, her robes and feathers surrounding her. She might have been simply sleeping, if not for the broken, twisted remains of the Lost Collar of Arboc around her neck.

"Well," said Osmuth. "What happens now? Guessing neither of us wants to be here when she wakes up."

Warden Pike nodded. "Correct, so now you will leave. I will seal this place when I follow. Then I will see what has become of my school."

"Vivienne'll bust out once she's back up to strength, you know."

"Yes, I know."

Osmuth licked his lips. "There's some awfully nice magic knickknacks lying around right at the minute. Mind giving me five minutes to do a little shopping?"

"You will not take Vivienne's things," rumbled Warden Pike. "I trust you even less with them than her."

"Flattered! But come on, can't tell me *you're* not taking a souvenir or two."

"Only what I must to keep my school safe."

"Not worried about the rest of Oz?"

"Vivienne is a tolerable threat without the collar. It is the Witch Council's responsibility to protect Oz. I will not do their work for them."

Osmuth let out a guffaw. "Ha! Classic Threnny. Wish people knew how funny you can be."

Warden Pike paused. “What is funny?”

The other man’s grin dropped. “Wait, you really don’t know? Really truly?”

“Know what?”

The grin returned three times as wide. “Oh, not telling. This is too, too good!” Osmuth shook his head. “Going to be laughing about this for decades.”

Warden Pike was tired and hungry. He was angry with himself for getting captured. And he was sick of letting his former friend get to him.

“You may laugh,” he said, waving both hands in different directions, “on your own time.”

Osmuth was lifted into the air and carried across to the nearest window, which was suddenly no longer there. Cold mountain air flowed in.

“You know you can’t beat wicked, Threnny,” Osmuth said. “Not forever. Not for good.”

“I know it better than you,” said Warden Pike. “And that has never been my intention.”

Another wave of his hand, and Osmuth Rust floated out into the night, the window reappearing behind him. Pike undid the holding spell, watching calmly as the man fell for three full seconds before transforming into a vestabird.

With a swoop of midnight wings and a final flash from one laughing amber eye, Osmuth Rust turned to the west and was gone.

Warden Pike let out a long breath, alone at last in Vivienne Morderay's lair.

Well, apart from Vivienne herself, of course.

He took his time looking around, exploring all the rooms he hadn't seen from his cage. Vivienne had always had a liking for the grand and precious and rare, he knew, so he was unsurprised by the opulence of her home. He was impressed, though, by the armory.

Almost all Vivienne's tools, weapons, and artifacts were known to him. Many were famous creations of witches of the past, others the culmination of projects Vivienne had started at school. He was glad Osmuth was not there to see his fingers twitch. Some of these treasures were hard to pass up.

As he passed a particularly over-the-top marble pedestal, the large sphere of lemon quartz perched atop it suddenly began to glow.

"Clever," whispered Warden Pike, testing the spellweave. "Emergency power."

In the next room, Vivienne Morderay gave a groan.

Pike flowed across the lair like smoke and knelt down beside her. The wicked witch's eyes were still closed, but color was coming back into her lavender face, and her hands flexed against the rugs.

Carefully, he reached out for the collar.

Even now, with the serpent shape fractured all the way

around, he braced for resistance, a brutal curse, some powerful defense even he couldn't see.

But his fingertips brushed the golden coils, and nothing happened.

Warden Pike fought down a shudder as he tapped the first of the seven gems in their rainbow line. He knew enough about this object to understand he should not have been able to touch a single one of them. There was only one power in all of Oz that could have done this.

Vivienne's eyes fluttered.

Quickly, Warden Pike gathered up the pins—the collar itself would have to remain—then backed away, taking one last look round before banishing the circling fire.

"Until we meet again," he said.

In another moment he was out in the night, riding on the wind. Raising his hands, he sealed Vivienne's lair in ice and darkness, snow and stone.

It would hold her for a while, he knew, but not forever. She would awaken, and she would be angry. But she would no longer have the full Lost Collar of Arboc. Her bite had been lessened.

Already dreaming of a hot meal and good sleep in his own bed—provided his school was still standing—Warden Threnody Pike shifted into a swift marbled eagle and turned on the frozen air for home.

By the time a great scream of rage echoed around the Hollow Mountains, he was already too far away to hear.

36
THE RIGHT PLACE

Ava thought Swickwit after the storm looked like something out of a fairy tale.

The night seemed extra dark without the fiery green glow, but lights had bloomed on every tower top, along with a fair number of magical fireworks, as the whole school celebrated the end of its captivity.

The steaming fog was back where it should be, rising off the boiling lake. The new glass hills shimmered behind it, reflecting the bangs and flashes as well as the whoops and cheers.

The Nettle students stood together on the edge of their tower, watching the teachers and Broom students being revived along the shore. The lake monster had vanished, returning to its home the moment everyone was safe, but plenty of Ava's classmates were still discussing it.

"We *have* to find out more about it," Wolfgang was saying. "That's the coolest thing I've seen all year."

"What do you think it eats?" said Opal.

"I want to know its name," said Branwen.

"Do you think it likes gingerbread?" Carmelie mused.

Ava felt a rush of affection for her classmates. They were

all very different people—wildly different, even—but she knew them so much better now. There would still be disagreements and feuds ahead, but she had a feeling their time in Nettle Tower was going to be a lot more fun from now on.

Henry caught her eye and smiled.

"That was intense," he said. "But do you think it's really over? Will Vivienne leave us alone?"

Ava shook her head as Crow and Tinabella leaned in to listen. "I don't know. We definitely did something to the collar. It *felt* like it broke, and the storm's gone, so maybe?"

"Viv still *has* the collar, though," put in Tinabella. "And the book, so she might be able to fix it. Either way, she's gonna be super, super mad."

Crow nodded. "Guess we'll just have to wait and see what happens."

"We'll be ready if she does come back," said Henry. "We've got Ava Heartstraw and Tinabella Grouse, and they're unbeatable."

Ava had only managed to blush at his words when Matthew shouted, "Look! It's Gern!"

They'd all seen Gern flying from tower to tower, checking on the other students. Now, at last, it was their turn as he swooped out of the darkness, landing with a thump beside them.

He got a warm welcome.

"Hooray for Gern!"

"Welcome back!"

"You were so brave attacking the storm like that!"

"Will you show us gargoyle magic sometime, please? Most of us missed it!"

"You have to tell us what it was like inside!"

"Why'd you leave us for last?"

The final question came from Dorian, and it set Gern, who had been waving for silence, chuckling.

"Watchin', were yeh? Well, I'm checkin' on you lot last 'cause yeh can clearly take care of yerselves!"

The Nettle students beamed.

"But no time now fer questions," Gern continued. "I can't stop. I jus' came to see you were all alive. The teachers an' Broom students'll be fine, but it'll take a while, so I'll be keepin' things runnin' again fer a bit. That means yeh'll 'ave to take care of yerselves termorrow. I know, I know!" Gern held up his hands. "I know yeh've got yer tests. But you won't need me. It'll all take care of itself. Ask Crow; he can lead yeh right."

Crow gave a nervous thumbs-up, and Ava's stomach did a little dance. How were they still supposed to take the tests tomorrow after everything that had happened? If there were any fairness in the world, beating Vivienne would have been enough to prove they were all pretty good at magic.

"Right, that's me, then," said Gern, and Ava noticed how

utterly exhausted he looked. “I know it won’t make a spot of diff’rence, but please be good. If I can’t make it in to see yeh termorrow, I’ll send Burdock once he’s awake.”

Gern turned to go, then stopped.

“Oh, nearly fergot. Ava, I’ve got somethin’ of yers.”

The gargoyle reached inside his stone tunic.

“Um, Gern?” said Tinabella. “How are we only just finding out that you’ve got pockets?”

Gern grinned, pulling out a damp wad of fabric. He shook it, and Ava gasped.

“My cactus dress!”

“Found it in the lake,” Gern said, handing it over. “Bit ripped here an’ there, but nothin’ that can’t be fixed. An’ it sure is clean after that boilin’ wash!”

Ava hugged the precious garment, not caring that it was getting her wet. “Thank you,” she said, partly to Gern, and partly to whatever magic had made this miracle happen. “Thank you, thank you, thank you.”

“So long then!” Gern called, striding for the edge. “Oh, an’ well done! You lot saved Swickwit, an’ no one will ever, ever ferget it!”

The class stayed on the roof for a while after he was gone, not wanting to miss out on a single thing as the school pulled itself back together. Eventually, though, yawns crept in amid the excitement, and the lights on the other towers began disappearing as the older students made their own way to bed.

Her eyelids heavier than she could ever remember, Ava followed the rest of her class back into Nettle Tower. It had been a night of terror and triumph, and somehow—*somehow*—she still had the biggest test of her life to get through in the morning.

The air in the Round Room seemed to fizz the next morning as the fourteen Nettle students gathered in a half circle, staring at the numberless countdown clock.

They had all risen late and powered through breakfast, doing much less talking than usual over their brambleberry cake, every face in the tower carrying the same bleary, anxious expression.

A warning chime from the clock set off a general scramble to get ready, and as the last of them scurried into the Round Room, there was a sudden *shwuck,* and every one of the doors—dorm, classroom, lab, and library—vanished.

"This is it," said Crow, swinging his arms at his sides. "The test should start in a few minutes."

His words seemed to break the morning's spell of silence, and nervous murmuring spread through the room.

"Do you think we're ready?" Ava heard Opal ask Margo. "We've learned a ton like Professor Mulch said to, but you never know."

"Who do you think does the testing?" Beryl said behind them. "Will it be the teachers, now that they're back?"

“I don’t care who it is, so long as Crow passes this time,” answered Wolfgang. “The poor guy totally deserves it!”

Ava listened, her own nerves jangling too much to join in.

Her entire future depended on what happened next.

Ding. Ding. Ding.

All conversation ceased at the three clear chimes.

A tall door set into the clock opened. Darkness loomed inside.

Everyone looked to Crow.

“Okay,” he said, taking a deep breath and letting it out slowly. “Follow me.”

Crow crossed the room and vanished into the darkness. Carmelie followed, then Henry. A rough line formed, and Ava watched Matthew, Jadis, and Branwen disappear. Then it was her turn.

One step, a moment of spinning vertigo, and she was through, suddenly blinking in soft winter sunlight.

She looked around.

She was in a courtyard tucked between stone buildings. She didn’t recognize it, but it could have been any of the hundreds of courtyards that dotted the school: a small clearing roughly the size of her house back in the desert, with cracked flagstones, weeds, and three rotting pigeons dozing on the edge of a dry fountain.

There was no one else there.

"Um, hello?" Ava called.

"Hello."

Ava spun around. The rotting pigeons were looking at her.

"Ava Heartstraw?" chirped the nearest.

"Y-yes," Ava answered. "That's me."

"Welcome to your Midwinter testing. Are you ready?"

Ava's mind reeled at the discovery that the rotting pigeons were the school's built-in magic examiners. But a little voice in the back of her head told her the test might have already begun, so she thought about her answer instead of blurting out a *yes*.

She thought about everything she'd been through—not just in the past few weeks, with the test prep and the storm and going full, actual wicked, but over the whole year so far, everything since that moment all those months ago when the messenger parrot had landed on her doorstep and told her that she had magic.

Becoming a witch had seemed like the grandest thing in the world back then, an impossibly glorious dream.

Now, halfway through her first year of magic school, she could say for certain that a witch was exactly who she was meant to be. For all her many ups and downs, the more Ava learned about magic, the more she felt like herself. And that meant that however many things she might have gotten wrong in her time at Swickwit, and however much there still was for her to learn, she was in the right place.

She was on the right path.

"Yes, I'm ready," Ava said to the three rotting pigeons. "I definitely am."

EPILOGUE

Ava Heartstraw gazed around her at the crowded, noisy Round Room at the top of Nettle Tower, feeling very, very happy.

She and the other Nettle students had spent the afternoon frantically comparing notes on their Midwinter testing, and they were buzzing with the sense that they all might have done pretty well. The rotting pigeons had surprised everyone, and there was a friendly debate going on about what else might be hiding in plain sight around Swickwit. But it was the fact that Crow remembered every moment of his testing that really had them celebrating.

Dinner had been ice cream, more flavors to choose from than ever before, though Ava went for Moon Smoosh and Fizzing Jasmine out of pure nostalgia. The older students were back to their loud and boisterous ways, and to everyone's relief they were steadfastly ignoring the Nettle kids again. It had been surprisingly uncomfortable being looked at by so many people, even from the safety of their own tower top.

There'd been no sign of Gern all day, so as nighttime drew near the Nettles settled in to wait for the visit from Burdock.

They had plenty to tell him. It was hard to know just how much the strange, friendly librarian knew about what went on outside his bookish domain, but each of them was ready to recount every last detail of their battle with Vivienne whether he knew it already or not.

"Oh, how fabrulous to see you all!" Burdock said when he finally arrived. "I hear you've been performulating wonders!"

Everyone began speaking at once, telling him about those wonders, but Burdock held up his six hands for silence.

"I am afraid I cannot stay and listen," he said. "I am helping with the recoveration of the school." The class groaned. "But I do have a special guest who I hope will not disappointify you!"

Burdock retreated into the shadowy library, his arms held out, and another figure stepped forward: tall, severe, and intimidating, dressed from head to toe in black.

"Warden Pike!"

Crow shouted the loudest, but the rest of the class was right behind, all awe forgotten as they asked the warden where he had been, when he'd come back, how the teachers were, and if he knew every incredible, amazing detail of how they'd worked together to save the school.

Warden Pike looked as stern as ever as he gazed down at them, waiting for silence, but Ava suspected he was trying hard not to smile.

"Yes," he said, when they'd quieted. "I was away when the storm hit and could not get back in. I decided to track down Vivienne, but in the end, someone got there first."

His shining white eyes settled on Tinabella for a moment, then Ava.

"Professor Mulch and the other teachers are still very dizzy," he continued, "but they will be back to work soon. Oh, and I am pleased to say you have passed your Midwinter testing."

A gasp filled the Round Room.

"All of us?" Carmelie demanded as everyone glanced at Crow.

There was no mistaking it this time as the corners of Warden Pike's mouth curled up. "All of you."

It was a good thing they were inside, because the sound of the Nettles' celebrations would have echoed clear up to the stars.

"You have also," Warden Pike said, raising a hand for silence, "broken more school rules, laws, traditions, and regulations than any group of young people before you. I must therefore congratulate you on being the most talented and troublesome Nettle class in Swickwit history."

More cheering followed this announcement.

"We're disruptive!" cried Branwen.

"And proud of it!" added Wolfgang.

"As you should be," said Warden Pike. "But do please

remember that it is no child's duty to save the world, however good at it they may turn out to be."

Opal put her hand up. "Okay, yeah, but it *was* kind of fun, though."

Warden Pike nodded gravely. "I understand. Discovering and testing your strengths can indeed be a great adventure."

It was a beautiful moment, Ava thought, looking around at her proud, smiling classmates, and it would have been perfect, if Tinabella hadn't also chosen it to turn into a baked potato.

"I guess we found out who got hit with that lost curse," Ava managed to say through her tears. The class was in pandemonium. Beryl was laughing so hard she had to run and blow her nose, and Jadis and Matthew were in helpless puddles on the floor.

Luckily, Warden Pike was able to reverse the curse, and even Tinabella joined in the relieved laughter filling Nettle Tower after an exceptionally stressful few weeks.

Still, something was nagging at Ava. Three problems had been crowding her head back when all this had started. Two were resolved: Her reunion with Tinabella had gone okay, as had their Midwinter testing. There was just one more thing she still had to figure out.

The group's focus had been scattered by Tinabella's transformation, and everyone else was busy laughing and chatting. Summoning up her courage before she could change her mind, she hopped to her feet and approached Warden Pike in the doorway.

"Well, Miss Heartstraw," he said as she drew near. "You did not destroy my school after all. You have made some changes to it, but it is mostly in one piece, so I must thank you for that."

"Um, sure, hi," Ava said, distracted by a small square ruby pin glittering in Warden Pike's lapel. "Can I, um, ask you something? Maybe in private?"

Warden Pike extended a hand in invitation, and Ava followed him a few steps into the dark library. A glance back told her no one else was watching.

"Okay," she said, taking a deep breath. "You probably heard all about the fight with Vivienne?"

"The older students and parts of the school have filled me in," said Warden Pike. "And I had . . . my own view of the event."

"Cool," said Ava. "Only there's something nobody but me could tell you, and it's that Tinabella and I didn't defeat Vivienne in the end. At least, it wasn't us that beat the collar." She held out her hands, angling them in the light from the doorway so the scars showed clear. "It was these."

Warden Pike went very still.

"I, um, got them when I was down in—"

"The Bitter Forge," cut in Warden Pike. There was

something new in his voice, a strange, soft edge that almost might have been tenderness. "I know."

"Um, yeah," said Ava. "And sometimes they sort of tingle? I've done a bunch of research, and Tinabella, Henry, and Crow have helped, but we can't figure out what the symbols mean, or what they do, if they do anything, I mean."

She was losing track of what she was saying, her words tumbling together under the intensity of Warden Pike's gaze.

"Even Gern and Moldy—I mean, the Moldy Horse—didn't know, and the scars never did anything at all until . . ."

"Until you were face-to-face with Vivienne, and she was using the Collar of Arboc against you?" finished Warden Pike.

Ava nodded. "Do you, um, know why?"

Warden Pike inclined his head. "Because that collar was made by the same hammer that marked your hands, Miss Heartstraw."

Ava blinked, feeling for a moment as though Oz was falling away from under her again. "The Nettle Smith made Vivienne's collar?"

"Yes, though it was not always Vivienne's. It was fashioned by the Nettle Smith as a powerful magical reservoir meant to be used for good. It was Arboc, another ancient witch and highly skilled jeweler, who later added the pins, turning it into what it became."

Ava's eyes flicked to the pin in Warden Pike's lapel.

"But then," she said, new connections crashing into place in her head, "if you knew this whole time that the hammer could stop the collar, why did you let Vivienne use it? Why not just grab the hammer and go after her way earlier?"

Warden Pike let out a long breath. "First," he said, "because I have never dared touch the Stinging Hammer. Second, because Oz is layered in centuries upon centuries of magic: everyday magic, world-changing magic, magic that does not yet know itself what it is. And the people of Oz are very much the same. I have learned over my long life not to decide about people. I knew Vivienne might be dangerous. I knew she was gathering the scattered pieces of the collar. But I chose to give her the opportunity to grow into something I did not expect. We should all get to decide who we will become. I only sought to interfere when it was clear she had gone too far. I believe I made the same choice the man who made the collar would have made."

"But how do you know what the Nettle Smith would have wanted?" asked Ava.

"Because," said Warden Pike, his voice unusually soft, "he was my father."

With a small bow, Warden Pike turned and vanished into the shadowy library.

Ava stood in the dark doorway for a long time, staring after him, realizing that no matter how much she learned about magic, and Oz, and her place in both, there would never really be an end to the marvels and mysteries she could uncover.

Smiling at the thought, she stepped back into the light and noise of Nettle Tower, where all her friends were waiting.

ACKNOWLEDGMENTS

Book three, and it's still actual magic!

Biggest thanks to my team at Scholastic for making these books possible: editor David Levithan, designer Maeve Norton, copy editor Maddy Newquist, publicist extraordinaire Brooke Shearouse, and genuine miracle workers Jalen Garcia-Hall, Chris Satterlund, and Sarah Jacobson.

Eternal thanks to my agent, Brent Taylor, and everyone at Triada US Literary Agency.

Humongous thanks to cover artist Teo Skaffa, who captures magic like no one else.

Massive thanks to my family and friends, especially world-class Oz expert Terry Blas, Eliot Schrefer, Natalie Lloyd, Donna Barba Higuera, Kirby Larson (with special thanks to Esme for asking the question that became this book's epigraph!), Caroline Carlson, Grant Alexander, Levi Hastings, Dave Wheeler, Justin Murray, Amber Casali, Lindsey Newman, Travis Osborne, Merlin (still a good doggo), Carleton Starr, and my favorite baked potato, Alex Kahler.

Thanks always and forever to Kate Bush and Ursula K. Le Guin for more inspiration than I can get through in a lifetime.

And thanks to you, dear reader. You are the reason I do this.

ABOUT THE AUTHOR

Will Taylor cast his third spell when he was eleven and still works for a chocolate company, so that one seems to have worked, too. He is a marketing writer, avid reader, and award-winning children's author, and lives in Seattle surrounded by all the seagulls and not quite too many cozy sweaters. When not writing, Will can be found searching for the perfect bakery and completely losing his cool when he meets longhaired dachshunds.

His books include the School for Wicked Witches series, *The Language of Seabirds, Catch That Dog!, Slimed* (writing as Liam Gray), *Maggie & Abby's Neverending Pillow Fort,* and *Maggie & Abby and the Shipwreck Treehouse.*

You can visit him online at willtaylorbooks.com.

EVEN MORE WAITS ON THE WIND . . .
KEEP YOUR EYE OUT FOR

THE SCHOOL FOR WICKED WITCHES

BOOK #4!